CU00868173

GOD
FAVORS YOU

TANNETTE CALDERON

BALBOA.PRESS
A DIVISION OF HAY HOUSE

Balboa Press books may be ordered through booksellers or by contacting:

Balboa Press
A Division of Hay House
1663 Liberty Drive
Bloomington, IN 47403
www.balboapress.com
844-682-1282

Print information available on the last page.

ISBN: 978-1-5043-9679-0 (sc)
ISBN: 978-1-5043-9680-6 (hc)
ISBN: 978-1-5043-9703-2 (e)

Library of Congress Control Number: 2018901239

Balboa Press rev. date: 09/10/2021

Publication date: 09/10/2021

Contents

Acknowledgments

I must acknowledge all the spirits involved in creating this book because without their communications there would not be this writing for everyone to read. They are looking forward to the publishing of their work to see how others receive this book and place value on their words.

I also acknowledge God and all his blessings he bestows upon us all.

In appreciation for her time, consideration and editing help during the editing of this book, I thank my daughter, Alissa Calderon.

Also, in appreciation in advance for her time and help during the marketing of this book, I thank my daughter, Linnea Calderon.

Dedication

To all those spirits/souls that participated in the creation of this book to deliver the messages that needed to be written and conveyed.

To God for all the wondrous work he does. Bless God from whom all blessings flow.

Also, to my grandfather, Simon, my mother, Florence, and my daughters, Linnea and Alissa, all whom I love dearly and will always have them on my mind and in my heart. I remember all those family members and friends that were a part of my life. We will always be connected by the loving moments we shared.

Foreword

I n *The Favor of God*, published in 2012, Jerry Savelle mentions a "notice of pattern" which he declared, "The favor of God was poured out before Jesus came the first time, and before He makes His next appearance, there will be a manifestation of God's favor like no generation has seen."

He goes on to write, "Some Bible scholars describe the last days as a period of time lasting approximately 2,000 years. In that case, if the last days began on the day of Pentecost, then we must surely be near the end of the last days."

Jerry Savelle points out several Bible passages and continues by stating, "We can see from these Scripture passages that a major restoration is on God's agenda for the last days. I've been saying for many years that God is going to raise up an army that will literally march into the enemy's camp and take back everything that has been stolen from the Church. I believe we who are alive today are part of that army, and I believe we will fulfill the prophetic pattern of favor that was established when the children of Israel plundered the Egyptians as God delivered them out of 430 years of bondage."

He continues by stating, "Just as Israel had to be committed to walking in the favor of God in order to break the bondage of slavery, we, too, must be committed to walking in the favor of God in order to live victoriously in these last days."

Jerry Savelle's book tells of promises made by God and a vast restoration that is about to take place and is explained in this book,

God Favors You. It has been stated by those I have channeled that "Many have prophesied it over the years, and it will come true. In some areas, it has already started." These spirits also explained that this restoration talked about in *God Favors You* is the same as that mentioned in Jerry Savelle's book and is an extensive rejuvenation of the world. They went on to say that they are known to many and have witnessed many restorations, but this one is a major rejuvenation to the world as they see it from their world and others they have seen.

These spirits made clear that there is much to do in the way of restoration and rejuvenation, and they are busy getting ready for that to happen. They indicated that much would be gained and restored, and it will start soon. The Lord is formulating the direction, and they are getting ready for a great revival of God on the Earth. "It is for everyone to partake and reconcile their thoughts to Jesus and God."

"The nature of man and those that stand with man are in question and need revitalization, and it will be done to God's liking on Earth. He sees and wants much change to happen in the hearts of man. It is time for great changes..., and so, it will be done. It is the beginning of a new era about to happen. So, rejoice in the knowledge that this will happen and very shortly."

Introduction

I have had various experiences throughout my lifetime, which led to an interest in different facets of the spiritual realm. A significant event began in 2013 when I was led to a medium to have a reading. The reading took place on November 12, 2013, or 11/12/13, when I was given suggestions and instructions on how to proceed with my life if I wanted to be happier along with predictions of my future. At that time and several years prior, life was not going along so smoothly for me. I was not in the state of feeling that my life was the way it should be. My days were stagnant, without much feeling of purpose or satisfaction. I felt stuck and not going anywhere in my life. I thought I was not utilizing my time and abilities well. It seemed like I needed a complete overhaul to bring me back into a world of feeling, motivation, caring, and some needed happiness. I questioned my life purpose and what I should be doing many times in my life coming up with no definite overall answer. This time was no exception, and I again pondered my life purpose. What should I be doing with my life now and going forward? What was my primary objective in life? Why was I here? What was I supposed to be doing? I wanted these questions answered in the reading along with other significant aspects of my life which were on my mind.

I had evaluated my life and was not satisfied with where I was at or my situation or situations I had experienced. I still needed direction. I knew my life had to change and for the better. I felt that my life would improve over time, but I kept questioning when and how can I make my life better. I thought of many things to do to enhance my existence and circumstances. I continued getting involved in anything that might do just that, which included taking more courses and looking for a new job that would carry my abilities and interests further. It is almost like trying to find your way in life, again and again, similar to when you were young discovering what you were born to do except there were added roadblocks to overcome. I am fortunate that my curiosity and longing for new information and engaging experiences are a part of my personality, which made my various transitions less stressful at times.

So, at some point, I finally decided to have the reading, which eventually helped, and positioned me in an entirely different direction, than what I was doing or where I was going with my life. I went over the reading many times trying to put the puzzle pieces together looking for a place, person, or an indication that would relate to the information given to me in the reading. I had to let the words sink into my head as to what the words meant and what I had experienced so far as time went on. Many pieces began fitting together after a long time.

I had to rethink my possibilities. I had to open my mind even more and look into what I had not considered. I had to review the advice over and over again since I did not know if I could get used to the idea of an entirely new and different direction that may or may not be suited to me, which is how I thought of it at that time. I focused on what I was told to do and kept looking for the next bit of information given in the reading occurring in my life. It seemed to just happen without any means of a demand that I would have placed upon it but did not. Sometimes the pieces did not come together the way I thought they would, but one thing led to another engaging development and then another where the path foretold if I accepted it was taking place. Because of the reading by the medium, I began doing more reading, research, contemplation, and meditation, which led to the writing of this book. I am still following this new direction awaiting the next experience and work that I will do.

The main content of this book was spoken to me by various beings. In other words, it was channeled. These occurrences have developed more so in the past few years to where I now communicate with one or more beings almost every day. Many people including me refer to beings as entities, energy, or spirits, and other descriptive words. These are spirits that do communicate as evidenced by their words in this book.

This publication has some explanations that you may not be familiar with, and that will provide you with more clarity about life from a spiritual point of view. There are many messages for all to read and consider. If you follow the directions and do what is suggested, then your life will positively be changed. I hope you contemplate their words carefully and think how your life can and will be enhanced. This entire book was channeled, and their words are meant to help you understand more of what is of a spiritual nature happening around you in this world. It also gives you insights as to the words chosen by these spirits to communicate to us.

You will note that there are many words and phrases in this book that are not common to the English language currently. Even though there are so many grammatical errors and types of errors in this book based on our standards of correct written English of today, I have kept all of their phrasing and words as they were spoken to me along with the grammatical errors. No words were changed or added by anyone except those words that were agreed upon by the spirits after the first draft was written. I feel that the authenticity of their words will relate their message(s) much better than if I or anyone changed them.

Any additions/changes are put in with parentheses around the insertion. Also, they use the word man, and I believe that is a general term for a human being. They gave me the approval to put in the insertion of the word woman so that we know they mean both man and woman or human being. I only put the word woman in a few places so not to overdo any insertions, and you can read without too much interruption the flow of their words.

— Tannette Calderon
www.tpcinsights.com

Chapter 1

Coming of Age

When will I tell you a story of life in heaven? It is now that I shall reveal the life in heaven for all to know and be satisfied with a tale of what is heaven sent to you and all who listen to the Word of God. I am marveled at the persistence of man(/woman) and his nature to seek out the Lord and be with him time and time again.

I see wonderful happenings on the Earth now and will rejoice in much that will happen later. We see the Light of God being shown the way in men's hearts and minds again. We see love blooming to those who seek the Lord and his wisdom. We can curtail evil to some extent, but it is up to many to visualize an Earth with love and comfort to everyone. We see it happening and starting to bloom once again in the hearts of many. We see love, respect, and joyful ways going to begin again once more.

Love is the essence of mankind's nature - to be loved in many ways, (and) to feel the essence of what God offers to mankind. Love is the beauty of the Lord and all who follow him as Creator, and man who worships him daily as we see on the Earth plane. We are always looking to see what man is seeing, doing, and believing as to his true nature. With God, we are all one.

We come to help in the many ways we know how to help and offer them to you little by little. We see all that you are, know, like, have caution with, have fear and doubt that hold you back. We see it all. We are aware of your shortcomings and say that is all right for Earth is a training ground for all there. It is a decision you made before and are carrying it out for all to see how you are doing with your tasks at hand. We see that you are all trying diligently to overcome what you have been placed to do on Earth and see where you will end up at the end of this life you have right now. We see that you struggle and want to become better in your life. It is so, and we recognize all you do and try to do.

Believe that love is the essence of life - to maintain it, nurture it, and be one with all. We can see how you love, and what you do to follow in the Lord's footsteps as his follower to epitomize all that contact you for a need or to help in any way you can. We see what you do, and how you do it to others and all life on Earth. We see what you can accomplish even in one day that you would not do without the help of our Lord and Savior.

He is there for you so acknowledge him and be with him in spirit, mind, and body. We assure you of good results in many instances that you come across even in one day. We see the results and know that you are all aware in some way of the true nature of our Lord. We know that you are on your way to becoming Christlike. We see it often and know that you are trying to be more like it says in the Word of God. We revel in your efforts and see what you can do in the future also.

Many seek out heaven. Many know of heaven already, but there are those who do not know what it is in heaven, and how it affects them on Earth. We see so much from above and witness your troubles. We are here to tell you of life-changing instances that occurred in heaven, and you can see what gifts people have walked away with. In time, you will come to know the true nature of God and all that abide in him.

We see and recognize your place on the Earth, and know that in any place you have work that can be done in good nature to all and everything you come in contact with. We are here to help with showing more to you and reveal(ing) all that is of good to you. We see you are interested in knowing the good you can bring to others in their state on Earth. We see all and know that you are aware of us also. We can see that you want to change and be more like a true follower of Christ on Earth. So, we shall start with a brief story of one spirit who lacked knowledge and peace in his heart.

His name is Ezikiel. He was known for his sharp wit and humor to all who came near him. He was a barbarian in times of old. He was confused to know how to act in front of people at times. He was only a small man with no wealth to speak of in his town of many. We see him walking along the road and looking at the countryside full of greenery. We see him about to enter a home to get supplies for a journey. He knew what he needed and obtained those things. He asked for more but did not receive it.

He began to question all that he came in contact with. "What shall I do? What can I help with? What is there for me to do?" He questioned everything and everyone about his true purpose to them or to his family. He shouted on the hill one day, not knowing what he was supposed to be doing on Earth to help. He cried up to God and was told, "Do not worry. You will be given what you need to do in due time." It was a time to wait and see what will come unto him, and then he will see what he is needed to do in different instances. He is(was) ready, but the time was not. So, he waited and began to think of all he could do for others.

He thought of helping with replacing roofs. He began to do that work. He thought of helping with the water supply, and he did that also. He was also in charge of horses and livestock at times. He was helping his community doing what he could to help them survive the cold winters and lovely summers they experienced in his land. He saw many who began to crawl out of the holes of darkness. He saw those who also lived alone and in rock structures come alive in the sun and of the people. He saw them walk again to help in the ways of the Lord that seek help with the mind and body. He was witnessing changes that no one could have imagined before.

He was like a light for those around him. He drew close to those who needed help and said, "I am here to help you with your problems if I can." He was open to doing what he could in certain and many instances for others that lived near him. This is a gift bestowed upon him through God in his favor. He started helping those that needed help in whatever way he could help. He was open to doing what he could even if it was a small endeavor. It was help to another.

God does not only give you a thought, or a means to help. He shows you that you can do it with just a little effort. He opens your heart to do what you are able and sees that you can do it before you even try to start doing that which he expects you to do for him and others. He releases the flowing of caring in the soul and body that enables you to think of things you can do for others without much effort. It is the start of a new beginning of becoming one with the Lord and what you were sent to do on Earth for others.

You can see that he is responsive in what you need when you ask of him. He is there for you even in the smallest of ways. He connects with your heart and soul to give you what you need in that time you are low and not discerning what you need to do. He helps in your nature to provide you with a change so that he influences you in what you seek. He is there for you in many ways. Be mindful that he is aware of you always.

We are here to help you understand the ways of God and how he interacts with you at times. He is known to many, and you will realize that you are one of many who come(s) to the Lord for help and receive(s) it daily at times. We see the struggle of those with so much worry and deception around them. We see what it is like on heaven and Earth, and see the difference in the life you lead.

No one is there to help at times, but we can help by our nature of willingness and love of mankind. We can endure much of what you cannot even begin to describe. We see and hear all that you do. We are your helpers, practitioners of life and what is possible through Christ, who raised you up to awareness and life forgiving properties in nature. We see that you are struggling and need help, so we are here to provide what you need from earthly things.

We see a man walking into a town by the sea, and he is wanting food. He is a traveler of sorts. He collects from others what they do not want and sells them to others on his travels. He is known to all as the man of trade, or the collector, or Jasper. He is not wanting much from you, just a token or something useless to you. He will sell it willingly for trade of other things and give you what you need in return. He is trading for your good. In return, he may ask for some food or drink, water, milk or what you can offer him, so he does not starve to death on the road. He carries a bag of trinkets, and household goods with him to show you what he has to trade with.

He goes along his journey witnessing those he meets and telling stories of other lands. He is interesting to many and has much to say to others who will believe in his stories. Seek him when he comes to the town, and he will invite others to talk also. He has a following by his side. He can accommodate many since his group is growing. He is of good nature and most loving type of man.

He helps when he can, but not always since he is limited to what he can do for others. He limits his wealth by doing only what he can do as he thinks it to be so. He has much more to offer others but has not the mind to believe it. He carries with him some misbelief or unbelief, and it causes him to be limited in his efforts. He is only doing what he can he says, but that is not true in the eyes of God. God gave him more power than he knows. God does not limit anyone to do only what you can. He wants you to do more. He knows you can do so much more. He is awaiting your thoughts to him and knows you will contact him at some time. He is waiting to hear from you.

Jasper seeks to trade and be happy in what he does. He talks to many people, and on his journeys, he believes he is doing much to help others, but God asks him to do more. God speaks to him in his quiet times of aloneness and tells him to journey further, and not be afraid to do so. He can help beyond his limits. He asks God what he will do there, and God replies, "You will know when you get there. I will see that you know." Jasper trusts in the Lord and ventures further than before. He meets more people of need and wanting. Jasper brings them goods and helps as he goes when he can. Jasper has extended himself to do more.

God is happy that Jasper confided in him and wanted to do more for others. He is always aware of your wants. He suggests you do more things, but you have to listen to the words that God gives you in those quiet times. He is there to help you do the next thing. He is your guide to the next things you will do in your life. He may even recommend them to you so that you hear his words to you personally. He is among you everywhere. He can also lighten your load so that more can be done with you as the doer. God's awareness reaches all. Come to the Lord, and he will lift your burdens again and again.

Jasper helps many, and the word is that Jasper has become a changed man. He is listening more. He is reacting to the needs of those who talk to him. He is placing himself as a doer in the eyes of the Lord. He is trying to get others to help and be more Christlike in nature. Jasper has become well known in his area and others. He looks to travel more and be with those who need his help. He lifts problems from others as God has done with you but in a different way. He is there to help as he can with his limited understanding and his limited ways of getting things done, but he is doing much in his way.

We recognize Jasper as a creature of love and ability in his own right, and so does God. He is doing what is needed in different situations. He brings people together to make resolution and gives freely to others who need it. He is of true nature, and God is happy with him. He is still doing his trade but has extended himself to do more and in another area, so that he has extended himself to reach out to more people, and help when he can. He follows what God intends for him.

There is another who looks to God for a word of help. He sits on the mountainside in the grass and rocks and sees the country below of town and pasture. He is a nomad with sheep in the hills to take care of. He sees much from atop the mountains and wants to do more than just tend sheep all day. He comes down the mountain and talks to the townspeople and says, "I am from above you on the mountain. I want to do more." But what is it that he can do? It is thought and prayed over. People begin to think of many things he can do. He can be one who watches for problems in the town; strangers, accidents, foul play, people in need, (and) people who want help. Is that a town crier? It is like a newsman, but more. He has the capacity to do when the incident occurs. He is a witness to occurrence of need.

His name is Burtal. He watches and waits for signs of change in others or new people not known to the community. He recognizes his worth by what he sees and then does later. He gives people an awareness, if they do not see it as it is happening, but find out about it later. He becomes the eyes and ears of what he sees and talks of it in earnest with honesty and integrity. He brings light to those who need to see what really is happening when they cannot see it. He learns much of the ways of the people in the community and expects that he is finally helping in what he can do within his nature. He is accepted as a truth teller and helps others to do more and better because he speaks of their truth also.

One does not give grace to others but witness that which they do. That is the influence one has over another. Your works or deeds influence the many around you daily. You can see your goodness in others by what you give them. They will always reflect you and your own nature, so be steadfast in what and who you are. Shine in your own glory among others.

Reflections are seen from others near you. We can see your good works, and it reflects on us also. We are mindful and can feel you and your works in your being. We can even feel your pain and sorrow. We are near to you daily. You may not believe in this, but it is so.

We can establish a need in you also. We can influence your heart to be a little more caring if needed. We have the ability to give you some of what you need spiritually. It has been done to many, and they realize the change in them. It is so. We have attained more abilities than you have, and show them to you as needed. It is what we do, and are asked to do from God our Creator. We help those in need but in our own way. It is not like yours in many ways.

We are here to support your endeavors, but you must ask and be heard by us or else we cannot help. We have helped many over the ages, and they have realized that we are real in nature, but not totally visible by you on the Earth. We see much and want to do more but are limited in what we can do to influence you in your daily problems, but we can do much.

Our times are different. We flow through the worlds and become spirit, light, and dust to those who wish it. We are energy in many forms if need be. We walk in the light and see the heavens as true spirits would do. We are of the nature of God in many respects. He is caring, loving, acting in his faith to you, and assured of what you need to do to gain your love for others. He likens to you as you perceive him to be so. He is all encompassing in the worlds of nature and goes everywhere with everyone. He is present. No one can say that they have not heard the Word of God spoken to them. He has revealed himself many times and in many ways. Were you listening for his Word? Did you recognize that it was him speaking to you? He has done it even while you sleep. He is present among you.

What can we say that you will realize it to be so? We can talk and talk about nature and living, but it is up to you to seek and hear his voice unto you. We know you can hear him. He has made it so. We know you can know him. He has made it so. We know you can be sheltered by him. He has made that so also. He is of your nature also. Wish it so, and you will have it brought unto you. Do it out loud so many can hear what you seek. These many may not be of Earth beings, but of spiritual nature. It is so. Be mindful we hear everything you speak, and it is recorded by you. We expect nothing less than to hear your voice as you need something from us. We can be there in an instant to save, help you, and care for you.

We are fighting to protect you in ways you do not know. We see all ills that become you even if you do not. We see all the struggles you face in your life. You can be assured we are willing to help you when you fall or need assistance. We welcome your thoughts and prayers of help.

There is none greater than God, and he is our leader. So be mindful to be assured we are around you daily. It may not seem so, but it is. We carry love and light to you. We can change your gloom to peace and serenity. It is so. We can fight for resistance and give you strength to do so. We have the power to change you in many ways, and it can be done. We will shield you if needed. We can make your happiness be heard around the world. We can say it is done to you, and it will be done just as if God spoke it to you.

His nature is pure and loving. Ours is more complicated, and it is telling of who we are and what we do for you and others. We are symbolizing our work as many with many duties that can be used in your favor. We speak the truth about our nature. We are asking for you to connect with us if you need us to. We are here to assist you. God governs us, and we are here to do what he wants us to do.

We are the angels of the Lord and can assist as needed. We have many duties and are always around in your time and space, but you may not see us until it is time for you to do so. We are here.

Chapter 2

Mission for Everyone

Besides giving of our nature to everyone, we can expand your feelings as we said to you. We have the power to give you expandedness as is willed by God. We see your nature and see you lacking at times. We can assist in this rejuvenation of your body, and it becomes you in nature to do so. We can heal you in areas unseen by you. We can allow others to feel your hurt, and be heard from those who cannot hear you. We see there is likeness in spirit, but what you endure is different in many ways. Life is a growing expansiveness and never stops in our realm. There is always life happening. It is never-ending.

Life occurs, goes, and is reborn in another form. It has always been so. We see that yours is of the same nature. We attest to the ever so repeatedness of this process. What can we say that will make you understand that life is enduring in nature? It never ends and is long lasting by nature. It encompasses so much of what is out there in space and time. Much is of not what you know, but it is there. You will know so one day. We can attest to that also. We liken unto you to share some of what we know and realize that it will need time to settle in you and realize that it is so. It will be done in time.

Today, your life is pleasant to some extent, and you realize that you are one in nature. Well, you are one in God and liken to him. He has made it so. He speaks to you in many ways, though you may not have recognized this to be so. He has opened up to you. It is now that you need to open up to him and make it so. We wish you to do so. We can expand you more than you thought so. We believe in your nature and its expansiveness. We are here to assist if needed.

Believe in your nature and what more you can do to assist others in their plight on Earth. We can see so much more good being done, and you can do it also. We are here again to assist. Just ask us for our help. Be mindful that we are limited, but have many gifts to share. The gifts can pour out from the heavens. It is of your favor if you are given a gift from God. We see it happening all the time with others and wish it to be so with you. We know you have the nature to expand and be one with God. He likens it to you and us. We know you can do this also. It is in your nature to do what we wish for you.

Atonement is a highly asked for request only by few. We can endure it, but it is God's will that provides this. He is the decision maker in this request. We are the subjects under his rule and do what he wants us to do. We are here to help in any way we can through his will and by his means. He lives in all and is all with one. He is one with all. He can hear, see, experience what you have done and can release you of your burdens if he deems so. It is of his nature to decide what is to be done. We endure for his will to be done.

You must know that he is the Creator and one who gives life to those who need it and ask for it. We are subject to his commands and demands. It is his nature. So as we speak, he hears us speaking to you, and can say if it is so or not. He tells us what to say and how to say it so we will be understood by you in your realm. We know this to be true. He allows what is heard and not heard, and by whom the information is given or not given. He hears all requests and can make it happen or not. He hears each word you speak or think or whisper to another. He knows you so well. He will be there if you ask, and it is his nature to give it to you as needed or when the time is right. Be not impatient when you connect with God in communication. He knows your needs and wants, and can hear you daily or all the time. He knows what you need. Believe it to be so.

He guides your hand even as you write when you are connected to him. He guides your aspirations in many instances. You hear him, and he does speak to you in silence. We are sure you can hear him at times. We know that he will help you in what you do or need to do. He is there as we said as needed. Be mindful that he is all around in everything you see, hear, smell, sit upon, walk upon, kneel upon, and dream to be, or have, or be. He is there listening to you and is watching all that is going on in you, around you, and with others. He endures all, sees all, is all, and yes is all. We cannot make it plainer to you. You can accept it as it is told to you, and it is so.

He can rival anyone to be put before him. He can make his presence known to you even as you speak to him. He is there. Do not be afraid to speak with him. He is listening all the time. You can seek him and find him anywhere you are. He is the atoms you drink, or breathe, or swim in, or look into the heavens and see. He is all, and all is one unto you to realize, that he is and ever shall be. Life endures because he is there. Love endures because he is there. He has plans, and that is your future in life and love. He maintains all and sees what is progressing. He lifts us and can bring us to his nature at his will. He loves us and is aware of what we are to him and what he is to us. Abide in the law, and you will reap the fruits of your labors. We are talking of God's laws.

God's laws besides his Commandments are varied in nature. There are laws that he has that are never failing. He has laws that require understanding. It takes time to understand all that God has created and why. We see more of his laws defining us, and what we can and cannot do. He can do so much with just a thought than you can do with your entire body. He is among all, and he governs all by his laws. It is best to know what his laws are so that you have a complete understanding of his and your nature. We acknowledge that he is all powerful and can take away what he has granted. It is so. Love and life endure though, so be not weary of this. It will always endure.

God is true to his Word. He abides in his Word, and we live his Word. We are accustomed to his Word by our nature. We cannot refuse to hear his Word. He lets us know what he speaks to us in many ways.

He lets us know of what he wants us to do, and why he has come to tell us.

We know he is of sanctified spirit, and it is within this spirit that we long to be nurtured. He gives us life, love, harmony, peace, endurance, compassion, caring, prosperity, goodness, and so much more than can be listed here. He is the one who is our Father in heaven that knows all and sees and gives all. He is our resource for all what we are or what we come in contact with. You cannot deny his greatness to everyone and everything. There is no one like him.

Can you not see God in a blade of grass? He is there. Can you not see God in a glass of milk? He is there. Can you not see God in the stars at night? He is there. He attains the likeness of all that you see and feel that is beauty and life, love, and so much more. He is the Presence. He is the one enduring. He is the life that is present. He is, and always will be. He is never-ending and never disposable. He maintains life and is life. It may seem paradoxical, but it is what it is. It is the truth.

Life forms may come and go, but God is there creating and maintaining life as it is in any form he deems to be so. It is his presence that maintains it all. We see his nature all the time in many life forms. You can see it even today if you glance at a flower or a rock. His power is in all and is felt by all. We know this to be true and right. God is and maintains all that we see, feel, touch, dream, aspire to, and endure. We know it to be true in life and nature - his nature.

Love is his nature also. He loves and wants to be loved by all. He speaks with love and likes to be spoken to in love. He guides your path with love and endurance. He makes it known to you that you are loved by not only him but by many. We see it daily. We feel it from others. We see it all the time in many details of love that are presented to us. He can be just what you want, and just what you need. His love is never-ending, and it will endure over time, space, and light years beyond the known. You can seek his love, and you will find it. That is the truth for everyone and everything.

He is known to all, and all know him. You may not realize that he is known to all, but he is. This is factual and capably said to those who listen. We endure, and he endures. We promote as he promotes. He praises and is praised. We accomplish much, and he does so also. We are not ourselves without him. We are with him, and he is with us. We cannot be separated from him by nature of likeness. We are one in the same. We are his, and he is ours. You can see this everywhere you look and feel. He is there.

Chapter 3

Be Knownst to God

(Several angels speaking to me are Ezikiel, Thomas, Benjamin, John, Peter, Paul, and others, all spoken of in the Holy Bible.)

When can we endure the Holy One in our presence? We can endure it all, and at any time. He will make it known, if you are required to be with him or not. He can speak to you with the slightest of thought, and you will know, that it is him. He makes himself known to you, and you will just know. It is as simple as that is to say it is.

God bestows gifts on those that are wanting to do something in God's nature. He realizes that you are just human, and not capable of everything he is, so he bestows certain traits on you or gifts that can make you capable of more than you were previously. He has the capability, and the right to do so. If you ask of him, he will do so, but in his own time and way. We ask assurance that it will be so, and God gives his assurance that it will be done in the proper time and way for you to realize, that which you are being given.

God's list of gifts is long, and it all depends on your needs, and if he is willing to give you something that you will need to handle. He alone decides on these things. You cannot win him over in any manner, but to wait patiently, and he will decide what and when to give you what you need by his will and your need and plan within your life situation. Be patient and endure.

Life stems from all, and all is(are) within many. We are so related, connected, and growing as one large energy field, so that the streams of life are expanding over and over, again and again. We see the presence it musters, and whether that be the will of God or something else, is determined by those involved. We can see it clearly that the oneness of God is the acceptable route to take. The experience to nurture is the most acceptable.

We can endure much, but it is God's will that gives us the endurance and ability to do so. We can do nothing without his help and never-ending care of us. We see it daily, and praise him for his glory and liken to him daily. We imitate what we know to be so. We accept what we have experienced to be right and our truth. We know so. We are likened unto him. We are following him, and it is so always. Life is bearable with those who care for us. He is there for us, and we acknowledge him and his ways of being there when we need him.

If you ask him for a resolution to your problem, it will come. It can come in many forms so be alert to what is happening around you, beside you, and just what unexpected thing might be happening. Heighten your awareness to receive it as it is. Awareness is the ability to be aware of everything around you and what is happening. So, this takes your focus on what is happening in the now. It makes you be more in the present for all sounds, thoughts, smells, visions, dreams, what people say to you, what you see, and even visualize.

What you are drawn to is important also, because one thing leads to another and another and before you realize it, you are being given something extraordinary in nature or not an everyday occurrence. It is a marvelous feeling to realize what is really happening, and no one else knows it but you. You are witnessing something so special to you, and you alone. It has happened and can and will happen if you open yourself up to this more meaningful awareness of thought in mind, body, and soul experience. It can happen to you if you let it be so for you, and you alone. It is fantastic in nature, and the experience is like no other. It is amazing grace in the now or moment.

The experience fills one with joy and loving acceptance of what just happened, whether that be knowledge, visions, understanding, seeing or even experiencing the truth, responding to someone who has no clue of the understanding you just received, and are able to verbalize, or the act of just knowing what is and is not true, or you finally realize you have the answer to a question that has evaded you your entire life. It could even be a healing due to faith and acceptance. It is all of God's nature, and his willingness to give to you and you accept it as it is. It is enduring these feelings of joy and contentment. You realize that God is present and with you. There is no mistaken that fact based on what you experienced. You are one with the nature of God, and he has given you grace in one of many forms.

You are attuned to him, and he recognizes your longing to know, or he knows that you are wanting to experience more of what God's laws are capable of doing in your life. It is all good and well to aspire and want all you can experience in this life to get you closer to God and all that is. It is a life journey you take and are willing to experience based on your belief in God, and all that he is. There is no other like him. There is no other that can do what he does for you and others, alike and dissimilar. We are all one with God and his nature. Blessed be his holy name. Bless God. Bless God's nature.

Much of what we experience is everyday mundane things, but when God gets in the elements of our lives, there is passion, love, understanding, acceptance, joy, and so much more than we had before God came into our life as a real being showing his true nature and what he can do with us and for us. We can do more for God also by believing in his presence and loving nature. He is there. He is there for you, and you should know that to be true. He is always there. There is no one like him. He is there based on his nature that is similar to yours. You cannot deny that you are of value to God, and his nature is of value to you. We are one in the same and ever-present in many forms for others.

Some refer to him as Spirit, and this is so. It is another name for God as Spirit. He can take many forms also. He is upon you, and you know it to be true. He is above you, within you, beside you and ever-present. He is Spirit, and ever-present.

After you experience God in his nature, and he bestows grace upon you, you will never forget what he has done for you. It makes you want more of the same. It makes you seek more of him and his nature. You change into a better being anywhere that may be. You change for the good, and it is inspiring that you want more of his nature and his presence. You want to be more like him. Your happiness evolves into being more like him. You become more like him. You are connected by nature, and by his presence within you. It is like a growing thing or a growth within you, and it is pleasant and remarkable to have it within you - this renowned Spirit of love and caring. It develops and grows by each passing incident that you encounter one who needs help and assistance to know God more and more. He helps with giving others direction, and that is a good place to work with a person - a clear direction to follow God's examples and his nature.

The experience of God's grace is like no other. It is happiness on fire. It is joy beyond what you know of joy to be. It is that what you wallow in, and do not want to give up. You do not want the feeling to stop since it makes you feel so comforted and warm as if there is a burning inside that has increased your heart and soul to become of the true nature of God. It is like your heart and soul melded as one and is enlarging in your body. It is a peaceful, warm inner glowing that makes you feel more radiant, whether you are radiating or not as others see you in the present. You feel what you feel, and there is no denying it is from Spirit or others commanded by God. It is from him and him alone that you receive what he offers, and you accept it knowing that it is from him. You carry the experience within you, and will never forget what you have experienced. He is within you, and you know it. There is no denying that he is within you, and you know it to be so.

Chapter 4

Make Your Day a Happy One

Y ou know you are on the right track when you get that same feeling again from God. You experience a joy in your heart. You feel that you are full of happiness and love in your heart. Then, you know you are on the right track to fulfilling what God wants you to do in your life. This is simple to understand. It is an enduring part of our nature aligned with God's nature.

It is an assurance to do what he asks you to do. He carries your good intentions and knows that you are on your way to victory in this lifetime. He wants you to do well, and succeed on your spiritual journey through this lifetime. He cannot ask for anything more since you are trying to stay on track in your endeavors and be pleased with the outcome of what you do. We are assured that you will do well when you follow the will of God, and his nature abides in you.

You can tell that you are succeeding when you feel so much better about the outcome than would normally be hindered from you if you were doing it the wrong way according to God's laws and restrictions. We see that you struggle in decisions on what you are doing or trying to do. We see it is difficult for you to stay on track with your endeavors or to come to a complete finished work. We feel that you can do anything you want or try to do. So, let it be so with you also, and think that way with all you do.

Let us start with knowing that God is with you always. He is there to comfort and guide you. He is there to help in his way towards you, and shelter you if needed. He maintains his directions are solid and upstanding by nature. He knows that you will succeed given the will to try and gain fulfillness in finishing an endeavor. What we can say to you is this is a way to think always. You can succeed in anything you try to do and complete.

There are many ways of succeeding. You can finish and be correct in all that you have done. You can be mindful of what you have learned in what you are trying to accomplish. You can be heartily warmed that you gave the endeavor a sustained work, and are completing the tasks as you go. You can be sure you will finish as time goes on. There is no deadline to finish a task as you see it in your time. There is not a time guideline to follow. The task can sit and wait, and be finished another time. It is of no immediate consequence to finish it right away. Time is not the factor. The factor is finishing what you have started and intended to do.

We all seek recognition in what we do, but that is of no consequence either. It is what you do, and how you do it that matters. What you seek is fulfillment in what you do; joy in the creation and happiness in spirit of what you are doing. Pleasure that you are doing what is of God's work, and that it is in line with what he wants you to do. You can be the initial spark of the essence of God's work for you. You will know if it seems right for you to do or not. Remember, he is guiding you and your path of many decisions that you make in your life. He recognizes your wants and knows the way of making yourself happy and aligning with him as you go within your journey. You are blessed in many ways, and that is to your benefit to recognize all that God is doing in your life on the Earth. He watches over you and others so that you can empower others to do well also. He is the overseer in lives of people. He does not abandon you at all in any part of your journey. He is there. Just ask for him, and he will be there for you to speak with him on your troubles.

God many times sends others to be of assistance to help you, and sometimes you can hear them with that voice in your head saying to go one way than another. Some even speak to you when you are not paying attention to what is happening or will happen to you. They speak so you can hear them. They show you what to do by words of actions you should take to be safe, and mind the moment you are in. You can many times hear what should be obvious to you, but you cannot see it. There are many who help and assist God. We are always here to help with your troubles and in bad times.

There are so many of us that are helpers to mankind. We see all the troubles and tribulations you have to endure. It is not an easy task you have taken upon yourself there on Earth. We have been watching many for many long years. We have been asked many times for help, and have given it freely. We see what is the nature of the problem, and work on fixing that part of it. We can see your choices, and adhere to the guidelines of what we can do or not do to help. We have restrictions also but are there to see what we can do to help in those times.

Life can contain so much beauty and honorable intentions, but if the task is not finished to your liking, then it will not be what you wanted to accomplish in the first place. Be mindful of what you first sought to do. Keep that in mind daily, and your direction will be solid and sustaining. You will complete what you set out to do. There is no doubt of this.

Maintain your goal. Keep it in mind daily. Do not be confused of what you want to accomplish. There are wonderful things to do on Earth. God is aware of all that is good, that needs to be done to fulfill your good choices, and be steadfast in working with others to complete what you started and will finish. He knows your heart and willingness to create a wonderful life for others. He sees that which you do not. He sees your spirit being lifted to new heights and realms in the spirit world when you favor in God's grace. He is watching daily as you go and accomplish even the slightest of menial tasks in his favor and yours. It matters that you work in the favor of God, and what he asks you to do. He is mindful that you can say no to his request, and that is your lawful right if that is what you intend to do. It is your nature to be of your own mind.

Your requests are granted, and you need to acknowledge that they are given to you so that you can proceed with the next thing to do. Recognizing God and you being in his favor are notable and pleasing to God. It is his nature. He accepts what you are given, and knows the struggling chaos of indecision you have at times. There are remedies for that. There are solutions to your ill behavior, so seek them out and gain your peacefulness back.

Be free of all ills, and thrive in your surroundings of love and light with the nature of God near you as you go through your life. Be accepting of others and their struggles for they are trying to accomplish something you may not have endeavored in your lifetime. They are on their own journey of light and love but have problems along the way just as you do. It is not any different. They are trying to utilize God, and be in his favor also. Most are trying with love and passion in their heart and soul. They want to be well with God, and those who have passed already.

They are your loved ones in spirit. Their nature is of loving those that they left behind. They have duties to perform and are busy doing those things that keep them in connection with the spirits in heaven. They work for them to do even not on the Earth. We work with them also and again abide by the guidelines set forth by God. Nature, love, and light are means to capturing what is of yours to overcome and do in the spans of a journey. There is always time to do what needs to be done, so you can accomplish your tasks that are right for you to do.

We can accommodate many, and work with so many that need our help. We are here then there. We fly like the light in a rainbow and adjust our energy as needed. We are overcoming restrictions to change what we need to change into so that we are giving what is asked for. We keep combining our talents with each other to get the complicated requests from being overbearing in nature. We see the light that you carry and know what is best and who to handle the problems you face. As a help, we can do much to assist.

We sustain ourselves in the light of the Lord and help others do so. We see that you are lifted to new heights within your thinking and aspirations. We see you grow in the light, and are welcome to do as much as you can in one lifetime. We see you do well, and see all that you have tried to do. There is no regret in your endeavors for you have accomplished something even in those. We know that you are always in a hurry to accomplish what is in your thoughts, but that is not how it is always done.

Stay on the path of good works than evil, and you will see such changes in you and those around you. Be astounded of all that you will see happen, and thank the Lord for all those blessings. You will see. You will know that he has worked on your behalf to ensure that you accomplish that which is good in nature. He is assured that you will do and make good of your endeavors. That is your nature also.

The tasks at hand are the most difficult because you need to start them already. They cannot linger and just wait. Your lifestyle does not permit many things to linger to be successful to yourself. You can see that your life changes in an instant due to some others misfortune and lacking. That is the dilemma that you need to overcome to get back to your tasks at hand.

What is lacking in man(/woman) and others; the lack of spirit, good intentions, primordial fear that should not be left to wander in your mind, and just the lacking of what you need to succeed? Is it an implement that you need? Is it faith to accept that you will succeed? Is it counterbalance in good and bad that is holding you back? Is it your nature of idleness that you have to overcome? Is it a means to set out on the journey in the first place? We can help in some ways for you to overcome these restrictions that you put upon yourself and think too much about.

We know that life's journey is hard and wearisome for many. We lack your nature but understand it. Be not complex, and you will succeed with those around you. Be not envious for those have skills that you do not have; work together to accomplish much. Be happy to face a problem together, and not walk away to some foreign place and leave the others behind to face the problems that you have the answers to. Jump in and be useful to others that need your assistance in their endeavors.

We can see much help is needed by each other on Earth and are here to tell you so. Be of right mind with each other, and be gracious in accepting another's help for it is needed in all cases of hardship and lacking. There is no lacking in what you have. It is lacking in what you give to one another that will help them. Be a part of the whole world's problem of living in the true nature of God and well-being to others that need some help. You can abide in their problems for a little while in order to fix some problem they may have. It is your nature to do good to others.

So, be what God has given you, and make haste to help those in some need, that you can offer to make them less miserable in their wallowing problems. They need assurance that you are there to help them in what they need to do for themselves. They are working on their life purpose also, but that may be different from yours. Your life purpose is a multitude of doings set by a taskmaster, which is your nature. You want to do much and accomplish much but stay on the task at hand. It is a journey of light and love. It is a sustained way of your life that is about your purpose on Earth. We can see your talents, and recognize all that you are as a child of God. He helps in your wavering thoughts, and indecisions.

Be clear-headed. Do not make confusing differences to lead your way. Be on track with your initial endeavor or purpose. It is a good sound idea that you are trying to accomplish. Stick with the endeavor no matter how hard it is. One day it will be accomplished in one way or another. It might not be the way you thought it would happen, but it will happen just the same to you. It will be accomplished in your lifetime in some way that you will recognize it to be so. That is a sustained journey with which you have set out, and it will be done to your liking at the end.

Many accomplish much, and many do not accomplish what they set out, but have they really looked at what they have set out to do in the first place? Have they sat and thought of the initial task, and why it was so that needed to be done? Ask yourself these questions, and see what you come up within your mind. It will be foretelling of what you have done.

Chapter 5

Watch for Others around You

Have no fear in what you try to accomplish. It is easier without the fear you hold onto. Fear is based in the mind and not the soul. It is a manifestation of doubt and lowliness; a perception of the untold, (or) a conjecture of the mind to those who think of all the outcomes that can, but won't happen. Be alert to negativity in your thoughts and be awakened to a new positive way of thinking that you will succeed in whatever you do. There is no doubt that you will succeed. There is no doubt to what you can accomplish even a fraction of the whole. You can do more than you think you can do. There is no doubt of this, and we hold firm that you can understand that it is so to everyone.

We are working to transition your mind to gain this understanding and hold onto the thought daily. Every minute you can do what your mind says you can do. It is the law and true by nature. Keep thoughts of good nature and positive. Life is blessed with positive doings, and this is so because you thought of it to be so. What others do may be perceived as negative to you, but it is not really since it is positive for them. Positive takes many forms, and you must be alert to these perceptions of others and yourself. Do not get dragged into thinking everything is negative and not a good thing for you. It is always a good thing to have aspirations to accomplish good in the world. You can perceive it and believe it, and it will be true to you. It will be true for you. There is not doubt on this.

What you can perceive is yours and yours alone. You have those thoughts, and it is because of your nature that you think of these things. If some share your thoughts, seek them out and decide if you are with (the) same purpose. Ask yourself, can I work with this person or that one that contains similar thoughts that I have. The goals may be the same, and on purpose or on task. Carrying much load on a large task is too big for one to handle, and you need help in accomplishing large tasks that are life changing in nature. The way to goals is through people and their efforts. It is like managing a large project for a company, but it is for you and your purpose. It is your mindset being developed and growing into a manifestation, that you realize is a work beheld by you in your mind. It is not in another's mind since your mind is working to create it as from you and you alone.

We see problems with similar minds and say that an individual has their own thoughts, aspirations, purposes, goals, and design of how their life should be done. So, when you get a thought write it down for you to go back to and develop yourself. Define what it is clearly so you can see your goal accomplished in the future with some help by others, or just yourself working on it. Write down your visions, your dreams, and your design that says how it should be or look like. These are all foretelling of what you are wanting to accomplish. There is no doubt to us or anyone that it was your idea then.

Life has a clear vision of you, and you sustain that is of your life going forward. You do not forget what you thought of years ago. You carry it with you to develop that thought. It never dies. It is within you that you take with you wherever you go. It sustains your movement and path. You cannot throw it away as carefully as you would like to. You keep it with you and work on it in some way over the years. It is there, and you know it. You trigger the thoughts you had years ago with a simple likeness of something that happened, and it will help to revisit that thought again. We are always on task with our thoughts and mindfulness of nature to what we want to accomplish in this lifetime. We are sustaining those thoughts to get them done. We revisit those thoughts again and again over time. There is no one that can copy our exact thoughts. They are unique by nature and connectedness.

Only when you speak it, do you begin to work on it. Only when you hear your words, do you have the mind to begin working on the matter. It becomes your manifested thought coming out of your mouth, so that you will realize it is time to start working on it, and you do it. It is done to you and for you. It is your nature to do so. It is the law to manifest your thoughts and make those thoughts happen in your life. So it is and will be now and forever. You are doing what your thoughts tell and want you to do.

There is no manipulation of data in your brain. It is still there where your body put it. There is no change in the initial thought. It is still there. You just need to accept it, remind yourself what it was, and begin doing what your thought was in the first place. It is still there waiting on your body to decide to do it, and the timing is of your purpose. The appropriate time in your life is essential in when you will start on it. It may not be today or tomorrow, but it will be done, and you will start on it one day. It never lingers but steps aside for needs and wants. It is thought, your purpose, that you carry with you. Life is a journey, and you take it with you all the time.

Be aware of those that would conflict with your thoughts, and do not get angry with those that do not aspire the same thoughts. You will accomplish them some day. Maybe not in the same way as you intended, but they will get done in one way or another. God has a plan for you, and your purpose(s) are in his hands given to you to carry out. He relies on your works to be meaningful in your life. He sees you want to do good and would enjoy to finish a meaningful task to help others. There is no doubt that you can do so much good in the world by a simple thought, which you will accomplish. It is the law and your nature to do so. God watches over you and relinquishes all problems in order for you to do what you are intended to do. So, be aware of your thoughts, and good you want to do in this world.

There is mobility in your soul, and want to go here and there to do what you can, but there is a time to just stay put, and do what you need to do. Do not be scattered in this and that without due cause and purpose. Stick with what you intend. Make it your duty to focus on the intended. You will be happier if you do this, and not wander in the darkness of forgotten purpose, but linger in the light of your own truth of why you are here, and what you should be doing. You will know this to be so by your happiness, and wanting to take up the tasks you think of. There is so much wanting, but is it on purpose, your purpose?

When do you know of your purpose? Is it like a flash of lightning in the sky? Is it a ray of sunshine in your window? No, it is felt deep within you, and you speak it to yourself often. You may not realize it to be so, but it is there lingering in the mind waiting to come out again and again to your liking. It may be dormant for a long time, and then suddenly it is upon you wanting to be done. It is like a ray of hope and happiness all in one. Such pleasure it brings to you when you may least expect it.

It may come in spurts of little thoughts of it; may be this or that over the years. I would like to do that and this, but it is not all consolidated in thought due to our bouncing thoughts on a daily basis. We think of things we would like to do in context with other things we are doing, but the form is not fully developed in our brains though we know it to be true - some truth to what we speak of. I would like to do this. I want to do this someday. I want to go here someday before I die. We all have thoughts of what we might do next or in due time, but it waits patiently until we are ready to formulate the best of all thoughts, which is on purpose to why we are here, and to do what we are here to do. It may be one thing or many things, but know that it is why you are here to accomplish before the end of this lifetime.

We see much and know of many instances when you know what it may be. We know you question your purpose throughout your lifetime. Eventually, it is revealed to you after much work and duties needed to be done on Earth. You may seek it, and know of it before your time. You may seek it, and discover it is the right time to start on this journey of purpose, and no longer wait for something else to happen so you can emerge forward in your need to fulfill your destiny.

When the time is right, it will begin to form and take place within your daily realm of activities. In those days, you will be delighted and happy that you have found that piece of silent plan coming forward to take hold of your head and heart. Your true nature is more appealing than it was before to yourself. You are on a task that is in need to be fulfilled. Every thought is captured and saved over time for this purpose. You have lived a life and now can endeavor to put the pieces together for another to be given the knowledge of your efforts, sacrifices, and longings. You are wrapped up in pursuing and fulfilling the need in you. You want it all to happen as it should. You are on purpose still.

Some know their purpose early on in life, and that is to their joy to look forward to being on purpose longer if that be so. Everyone is given their purpose in the time frame suited for them, and what they need to do in their lifetime. Some have more than one purpose to fulfill, and that makes their life more interesting, I suppose, by nature. We cannot say what is your future, but we can say that it is purposeful and well-meaning to all that come near you, and are given the fruits of your endeavors. Many know their purpose when they are born and are happy to continue to seek fulfillment in that purpose. Many know what is in store for them, but if it is not so or not in joy and love, you can change this. Problems linger but are easily wiped away with the hand of God near you.

We are all one in being with our Lord, and he shelters us constantly. He is aware of what he has given us to do, and we shall hope of his goodness and grace upon us in our endeavors. We seek him daily and wish all good upon everyone and everything. It is our destiny to help, and abide within the laws he has created. We are chosen to help in different ways, and we do so as told to do.

We accomplish much in the work of the Lord and seek to do more. It is our task, and he is our taskmaster. We do it rightly and justly. There is no other like him. We fall on our knees in praise and glory of his presence and of his nature. We are true to his needs, and no other shall come before him that he cannot command. He is just and firm and likens to be joyous and pleasing to all in his way and within his laws. Righteousness is his level, and we abide by him. There is no other like him, and we praise his glory for all time.

Chapter 6

Permit God into Your Soul

Time is us wanting more to do to complete what we are born to be on purposeful tasks. We want more joy and meaning in our life. We feel the happiness we received to be one with the Lord or the connectedness of being aligned with the Lord. We are similar and happiest when we are in similar tasks with him. Our joy is fueled by his delight in us.

We fuse our energy with the Lord and are enhanced in nature by him. He sees us loving the feelings we get from him, the joy of giving, and articulating what he wants us to do for others. He knows when we are on task with our purpose, and aligned with him. He is happiest then for us to complete our purpose in that lifetime. We work toward for that end.

We enjoy our many accomplishments in each lifetime and go forward with the knowledge to another life that we chose. We expand our awareness and give thanks to the Lord in helping us reach our goals to be with him and near him. He is an overseer of all who walk(s) in his footsteps. His glory is seen and favored by us. We yearn to be like him. He has authority over all and keeps alignment within each and between each.

He harkens to the angels what is expected, and they carry out their duties in alignment with everything. It is a complex and intricate system of a fined tuned frequency with which to create. We should be happy that we have such a heavenly goal to attain. It should be joyous to everyone that we are striving for such a highly tuned being with the Lord. There is no other feeling like the one we get from the Lord happening in so many circumstances. We initiate. He responds. We respond within our true feelings, and he shares his guidelines and reveals his ways to us. It is a communication like no other except for other spiritual beings. There is similar interconnectedness at times.

Many have chosen the similar path of walking in his shoes, and that is a difficult road to walk. There are many dangers for your spirit. There are many collapses possible. You must be strong in nature and your belief system to know that you can overcome anything. It is written in the laws from God. You have the capacity to not dwell in the darkness of untruth, deceit, and all those bad feelings that are not of our Lord. Be mindful that you are with one in the Lord for his is good. He is great. He is the Divine. He is with you wherever you are. So, the mystery of his goodness is reconciled to you again. Many have pondered that question over and over, again and again, depending on what happens to them. They doubt God's goodness in their life. It is always so. He has not changed. There is always light emanating from him and those around him.

The light is from the Creator, and for the Creator. It is his essence for his is life. He executes life to be, and it was and is. There is no denying that without God you would not be. You would not exist as a being to do what you are intended to do. There would be no you. The power of God is alive and real, and will always be. It is his purpose to be for anything that needs him.

God is subjected to profane words, name calling, dyer needs and prayers, and other hurtful thoughts which are not true to exist as such. God was born in a burst of power in the stars. He claimed his position by the sheer power of the explosion that made it so. It was a foretold destiny and was explained much later in the years. We have no definite writings on this right now. We seek guidelines on what to say or not say.

The explosion permeated the sky, and its particles were everywhere. They formed what we see as a formation of rocks, planets, and other substances. The actual cells and other components inherited the elements, and we maintain those elements today. We have diversified some, but that is the nature of growth. There is no stopping what has been put in a reaction. It will continue to do the same for a long, long time.

The Spirit was formed when we became a useful entity and interacted with many things. We were relentless to find answers to questions. We discovered our nature in a flash, and it became one with the Lord. His particles are our particles by his Law. We are still in his care and linger to hear everything he has to say to us. We try and mimic him, but it not always works.

The Great Beginning was of profound knowledge. Its expanse was great. Its destiny of a ruler, and of formidable size - he made it so from another time and place. He made it of an appearance of profound light from darkness. He is the Creator of all that you see and experience.

He is here and there. He is everywhere that you can imagine. He was not found under a rock or in a tree. He was always there and formed the rock and the tree, and was then there within the rock and the tree. His time was to be there to create, and see what he created. It was his glorified time that you know. No other existed before him. He was the placement of the stars. He was the position of the planets. He is in all and is all. He formulated everything from himself and is contained in it all.

The other place is his Kingdom in heaven. He has attested to his place from where he comes from. He fashioned the Creation from what is in heaven. He created colors beyond belief. He created all types of formations that allow growth and functional life. He created the wonder of the Creation. He built what you observe to be. There is no other that can formulate all, and still be within all. It is self-reliant what he made. He sparked creation, and let it flow within and out of the things created. He creates expansiveness to allow growth and room to fill more within what he has created. He acknowledges all that has been created and is connected to all. The link to him is through heaven where his Soul, the seat of the Soul, resides. This creation ability is just one aspect of God and his wondrous deeds.

His aspects are formulated by him. He shares with everything. He gives everything to all. He partakes and rules. He decides and pardons. He allows and hastens to withdraw. He is a power that has power. He is enumerable and develops more than you know to be. He is like a multiplying effect and deemed it so.

He took his attributes and gave it to us, to everything, every being, everything you can think of. He shared himself within his creation(s). He is formulated by a mathematical equation in that he can take those numbers, and make them mean something to everyone that wants to know. He has created it and knows of it. It is from and within him. He hides not from all he has created. He can be called the All-Knowing in that he knows of it all and always will.

Numbers are the key to understanding a small aspect of something. Numbers can connect you to knowledge of many things in the stars and heavens. Numbers can give size and shape, and determine the next sequence of what is to come from that you have extrapolated.

Numbers are a guide in a sense of what is to come or to be formulated next. Numbers show growth and many other aspects of things. It is a definition of a thing as it exists with part of the definition of that thing you are wanting to know about. Numbers help determine what it is, what is likened to it, what is its purpose, what it can do or not do, what it can mix with or not, and what we can do with it or not. We all follow the numbers to help with defining a thing.

We are numbers but of a different value and arrangement. Sequencing helps make a definition more workable to know what is meant. Numbers carry much information about the object and carries a significance to other objects. Numbers connect all to each other. It is like a puzzle waiting to be defined as you look at it changing again and again. It is like a moving target defined by numbers. It appears, changes, and then is somewhere else in time and space. You are watching the performance of everything as it moves through time and space.

See the relevance of something in numbers as it changes into something else. Where do the numbers flow to? What numbers are given up to create something else? What numbers flow in and out of something, and alter its state of matter? Numbers are of the definition of that object. It is defined in several ways, and it needs to be observed to understand more of what it has to give or not give to another or another state. Numbers show exactitude of the object. It does not give life to the object only describes it.

Chapter 7

Amaze Yourself with What You Do

God has created all. He utilizes space as a formulation, and then allows creation in the space. The formulation is a creation in his mind, so to speak, to where and what he wants to create. It is like a page on a computer asking for space. Given it, he can create what he wants and utilize as many more pages as he wants to use. That is similar to where you are in your understanding of what God does.

He can create or delete to his liking. He sets the rules of the page and those who access it. He works on refining each page to his own liking. He communicates from his command. He interacts with those on that page. He creates those on the page, allows or disallows access, and creates the page and pages to be in the same or similar mindset as his. He formulates, defines, creates, and shares, all in one page or those other pages. That is an abstract way of looking at what he does at times. When you do what he does, you are mimicking him, and he enjoys the process that you are creating too. He has given you the process to create in not only one way. Enjoy the art of creation for it is good in his eyes.

God enjoys seeing you do some of the most creative works. He likes to see new inventions or ways of thinking, or ways of how you figure things out and connect all the pieces to form something new to your standard of creation. He sees your progress and is there with you to help spark a thought that may be useful one day. There is much to keep you busy in the art of creation. There is so much that can be done.

Contemplation requires sparks of energy to fuel the creative process. He gives you those as needed, and if you want them. He touches your heartfelt yearnings to create something new and allows that process to take place in you and around you. Your creation is valuable to him, and he is aware of your lingering abilities to want to create more and more each day. It is a process he is well familiar with. He thrives on what you thrive on - the satisfaction of creating something beautiful, and useful to all those around you. What is more godlike than a creation? What is more captivating than a spark of a different energy created for a purpose? It is divine in nature, and it is all connected to what is and what is to come.

It is your creativity that creates usefulness to you and those around you. It connects you all to a new level, new understanding, and new place to be in mind, body, and spirit. You have risen with what you had, and formulated something else to give rise to something new that is useful to what is next to come to you and others. It is of proper sequence to have this going on with you, and to others who you do not know of yet. It is your ideal process of connecting to others beyond where you are also.

Connectivity for the good of all is what we are speaking to you about. Connect and be happy with each other and all. You can see in your mind what we are speaking about. It is there for you to understand what you are to do next and then after the next thing that you aspire to do. It is there in your mind and heart. Believe in yourself for the energy and spark is there within you to use and connect to others around you and in the future. They await for your idea or creation to inspire them to do more good, and spark the light in others too. It is a never-ending process that all can be a part of - creation for the good of others.

The future is unfolding for you to benefit many in your realm of Earth; much to be discovered and understood in order to go the next step in creating more good for many more to utilize. Other beings are struggling with their problems or misfortunes. They too need to progress further and be like-minded in purpose to align with God the Creator. The sharing of what we know is in the futures of both your realm and that of others. It is not to be spoken of yet, but it is coming one day. Necessity dictates you take care of your realm first and then aspire to move out further from your realm to be of good to other beings.

Their assistance to you is in the future, not now. You need to handle your problems and adjust to the problems at hand. There are many in your world right now and need attending to. People need to realize that we are all one in being with the Lord. What we do affects him and his realm. We need to aspire to his mindfulness and nature of creating, giving, sharing, and being present for one another. That is useful in order to proceed further with development outside your realm.

Corruption focuses on greed and self-indulgence. Name calling focuses on ego and showing off in a way that belittles the other. Stealing is of want. Lying is of black heartened ways. Your heart is not whole. All can be fixed and redeemed. There is no need to do all these things that darken your spirit and others. Read and learn about God and his ways. Many know of the Lord, and what he is and is doing for others to become more like him. Choose a path of enlightened thoughts to bring you unto the world of the Lord and his goodness. You will see how your inner thoughts change, and you will find peace in those changes since it likens your heart to more like his.

There are many mysteries of the Universe awaiting you, and when you open your heart to his, you will find some of the mysteries will give you great pleasure. You will then understand more what it is like to be in the workings of the Lord, our God. Blessings will unfold. Trust will be your guide forward. Life will be your choice for everything. Contemplation in the Word of the Lord will be your first thought so that you will better come to know the Lord, our God. Virtues will abide in you, and people will know that you are a follower of Christ the Lord.

Wisdom may be given to you. Caring will develop. Your heart will open to others, and they will open to you. It is a wonderful thing to experience among others and yourself. Falling into love with everyone is a fantastic experience that is associated to the caring of the country, or the city, or the community. It is a beautiful thing to witness and experience.

People respond to love and its pleasing feelings. They just grow and grow in others as you do good. They see you and respond in kind. Much love is needed to heal the wounded, and you have it in you to do just that. You can heal and be mindful of others and their plight. Heal the sick. Heal the poor. Heal the misguided. Heal the unknowing. Heal the reckless. Heal the fractured in nature. Heal the broken from others. Heal all that you can heal in others. It helps the world, and others and those around those that need healing.

Be a light, and show the way that others can follow and be whole again ready to do God's work in others. It grows and is never-ending. Much is experienced when you let a little love out to others, and they are recognized in that love and can allow love to be given by them to others also. It is just there waiting to happen.

Just tune into love and what it will do for others and you will see it right before your eyes what a little love can bring to another. It expands and grows just like that creation you are about to develop. It expands in others and grows like a flower in the field. It is a beautiful thing to witness; much love in your creation, whatever it will be. Timeless creation is what we aspire to, and you have the power to create that also. Keep showing love and responding in kind to another's love, so that you may know endless joy. It is our wish that you be given much favor in your endeavors.

Chapter 8

Pleasantries Are All about You

What is the return of love? Timeless times love returns in different forms, and it is amazing all that is done in love. Love is nurturing, caring, accepting, passionate, enduring, providing, managing hard tasks for others, creating a spot for safekeeping, tenderness, and so much more. Love is never ending in what we witness with others, and ourselves in that replenishes us and nurtures another. It shows our feelings in daily responses with others. We can see it everywhere we turn to look. There are these patterns over and over again.

Sometimes, an unlikely occurrence happens, an unknown happenstance, and love is there too. It is where you would least find it, and where most would find it. Love kindles the yearning to help another, and do it so that they respond eventually in a like manner to others. It repeats and repeats all the time. It is like a mathematical equation that is infinite with all the being generated again and again no matter what.

It just takes a person to unlock the feelings or to understand the situation to do a direct action to show someone, that there is caring out there in the world we live in. Life is occurring with love as a means to help multiply the matter of feelings to show another there is(are) actual feelings behind an action that another has to show someone, that it endures in many forms. It contains the spirit of the one who gives it and relates to the other spirit, that it is there in a caring fashion to help in some way whatever can be given at that time. Love is the communication to another that I am not going to harm you at that moment in time. Love is subtle, and it can be alarming. Love is shown in so many ways that you cannot count all that is done to and for you even in a day.

Thoughts of love are everywhere floating in the Universe. Love wishes passing all around you, and you do not even notice their appearance to see that they exist. Love can be a thought to another when they think of someone. They relive a favorite moment with that person in their mind, and it jumps to the other person with joy and lifts their spirit. It can be done, and you would not know from which it came. It is sent along the waves of the plane, and it is not obstructed by anything of matter. It shows that the existence of thoughts is surrounding all and affecting us all. It shows that we are in the midst of what others think, and what they say. It floats and points to the one in regard, and it moves in that direction so that the person or being gets the opportunity to feel the message sent. It knows where it is going and is directed in that direction. No need for a postage stamp or a computer to tell it where to go. It exists as you do in this world.

Thought is a force that we have some control of in the nature of our being. We can contain it, or send it along to another. It can be a driving force or a restricting force in that it affects the being it is directed to. It also does not have to be a being or alive, but it has to exist. Force can be a powerful weapon to ward off evil in others. It can be a seed sown in another's soul so that their heart can be changed or altered to be more accepting or loving to another. It is that which you desire to make so within another. You are changing them to be loving or not. There are many negatives when you talk about the unloving words or thoughts to another. This is manipulative and can be taken the wrong way even though not meant that way. People are translucent in the realm of thoughts. They pick them up like sponges in the sea. It floats around you, and you just let it wash over you good or bad. It permeates you, and it affects you. You can see changes in others all the time due to words and thoughts of others. It is like a washing that seeps into your skin and affects your being. You can see how people change over time.

Love renews, flourishes, regenerates from someone to another. It is passed along, and it grows where you plant it. You can send it, give it, say it, and in so doing affect another as if they heard you, or have access to it another way. It does contain the vibrations under which you sent the message. It has an underlying frequency that can alter your frequency. Changes are constant and occur all the time whether you know it or not.

You can pick up on subtle changes if you are sensitive, and feel the shifts of the energy or frequency from another, but many times people do not recognize this. They are unaware of what is really happening. They assume it is a bad day, a headache, a tired spell, or even just having a bad day. None are correct. It is the effects of others upon you happening right that instant. What you feel are others bombarding you with their thoughts, feelings, good wishes, and intentions towards you. You can feel it all eventually as it comes to you. It affects you and changes your mood, words, thoughts, and feelings also.

You are dependent on some of these messages and words to exist in good nature. You have to have some time in another's consciousness to be permeated with their thoughts. They will come to you, and everyone hopes that they will be loving in nature. Life carries forward in many different forms. There are spiritual levels you know not much of, and we are here to help you along to find out more about these realms that are all around you that affect you. We stand by what we say and acknowledge that you are possibly only first reading about this, but it does exist, and it is real.

People feel many different feelings all the time, but are unaware of why they are having them, or what these feelings mean. Feelings that may pinch your arm, harbor a headache or cause your toe to twitch, they are happening for a reason, and not all may know what that reason is. We are under a cloud at times to know what is really happening to us. Our awareness is low, and we think in terms of what is around us and in front of us, not what is all around us that we cannot see, but it is there to affect you in many ways.

We are of a victim's realm until we change all the bad to good. All our thoughts are like beacons to another. We see them in our light and share with them in our own way, and we divulge it all to another by our thinking and with words. Be mindful that you have much power over another being. Take your thoughts and words seriously, since they affect much around you always.

Even the blade of grass you walk on knows your intent. The trees and animal life knows your intent. You need not speak it to them, though positive, good words are more beneficial. Thoughts suggest what you are about, and what is your true nature. Other beings, animals, (and) plants can pick up on these thoughts and are affected by them. It is their nature to have some awareness of what is around them also. They know what is to come from another. They do not depend on your words to tell them what is going to happen next to them. They know already before you do the deed. They were given this so that they can adjust to their surroundings as they see fit. It is not a contemplative act, but a knowing to adjust within their surroundings. They do what they can to avoid a negative act towards them or others, but cannot always change the intended outcome.

Rocks, mountains, and those types of things have a low frequency to intentions, but they do have some knowing of what will happen due to the frequency of another nearby. It is their change of frequency that could be altered by an act done to them. They have some awareness of the intent and outcome, but it is not as great as the other forms of life on Earth.

We all have a place on Earth, and this place we are in changes over time. We move and go somewhere else due to circumstances. That is the same for plants, rocks, and things. We are all needed to be somewhere else for another reason being set forth upon us. It is the way it is on this planet. Life exists because it never fails to react in some way to an outside source whatever that source is. We are changing what is, and others are changing what is. We are all moving, reacting, and people are giving everything something else to react to on Earth. Plant your seeds wisely, because tomorrow will be the growth of what is done today.

Chapter 9

Partake in the Offering

Man(/Woman) is immortal in spirit and wisdom. He carries with him untold knowledge to other lifetimes, and he foresees the future as he goes. He is constantly thinking of new ways to do something; create something advantageous for others to use. Not only is man ever-changing, he is changing others and things around him. He takes what he gets and molds a new creation for others to witness, use, and behold unto others to use. He is creativity on the go. He moves to the sound of what he needs to do in life and does it well to his present ability.

He is restricted in what he can use or not use in this lifetime based on previous agreements with the Lord, but he does what he can and pushes forward in thought, ambition, purpose, driven motivation, and the capacity to see into the future of his own life and what is to come. Man is awaiting always the new and the relevant for the world to see. Man creates and gives to the world what he can at the time. He molds the plastics and enters new design in products not yet created. He is always thinking of something new to create, and pursue along with others that are in similar mode.

What one man can do is remarkable in that you see so many ideas flowing from someone, who has been given the fight of creation from the mind and using tools can do wonders to project the idea into being. It is a marvelous ability that some people have, and use it wisely. It is of a godlike nature in that it is creation on the move and from thought, action, deed, and words to others. You can create so much. It is all possible with your ideas, and temperament - foresight into the future of what you want to make and do for the world.

Time is of no value when you are creating. Time does not exist for those who create and feel the moment their thoughts of what it could be from their brain to paper to a model to the real thing from the drawing. Life is ever growing and expanding on the Earth so that wisdom flourishes. It is a cycling of thoughts back and forth, and creation enters to spark that thought and to carry out the deed of creation. It is a marvelous thing to watch in another person. I can see you know what I am talking about.

We acknowledge methods of sharing our thoughts to you, and you use them wisely at times. We help with your process and sometimes give you a boost of wisdom to help along the process you are in. We see to it that you do not stray too far from the intention of what you want to create. It is our duty or responsibility to help you along your process, and help materialize what it is you want.

We are here to guide you in your endeavors of all types. Man is not alone in his endeavors or wants. We are here to assist in your development for the glory of God and all his creations. We see you struggling with many ideas, and those that sound ready to be put to paper shall be done either by you or someone else. Life is sharing and caring of those that want to do so with others. We are here to help as needed again I say to you.

Most do-gooders are connected to the good of others. They are assembling to help each other whether that be in prayer, problem-solving, worship, praising God and all that he does. People are collecting themselves to do something on the Earth for others. It is the way of truth and light. We assemble to show our unity to the Lord, and his good works be done unto us and others. We come together for a purpose and vision, and we take our thoughts and feelings to others so that they can understand why we are together in an assembly.

We do that in heaven also. We assemble to give praise to the Holy One, God our Creator and Manifestor. He shines light on us so that we can experience his light to the fullest. We take the light with us and transform it to many things that need to be done for others. The Light of God is an enormous pleasure. It fills our souls, and bodies with everlasting warmth, direction, purpose, healing, and motivation. It straightens our problems and issues out so that we can see and feel straighter and less crooked of a past thought that needs fixing or straightened out by us. He cures us from our mistaken thoughts and feelings. He guides our thoughts and creates those feelings of love and awareness that he holds for you. He gives you this gift so that you can expand your life and purpose on Earth to others. He is anointing you with his grave/gift and sees that you are worthy to take yourself to new heights in your work for him.

He has more purpose and things for you to do on Earth and is showing you the care he has for you. He will not let you fall under his care ever. He knows what you are capable of, and what you can do, and what you have done in all lifetimes. He sees you expanding in this lifetime to know him again and again, and show others what you know and what you have experienced with him and other spirits.

He is giving you a gift of warmth in the feelings of his love and divinity. He heals you where you do not know you need healing. He anoints and heals your body to let you realize that he is there with you all the time. He gives you this and expects nothing, but wants you to be lifted more to his realm of sharing and doing good to others. He gives you that extra boost you need to accomplish what you are here for. He has lifted your spirit and healed you at the same time. He is all-powerful and anointing. He is the Anointed One.

Not everyone receives these gifts but those who do, remember the time they are given it, and never forget the warmth of the feeling and the healing nature. It is like a Utopia of feelings. It sends you higher in your spirit level. It raises your spirit feelings like lifting yourself higher in openness, gratitude for others, wanting to help others, planting the seed of giving, nurturing, radiation of being from the inside out and letting others see that radiant you.

It is for those who have needed to be lifted and told that they are on the right path to be a spokesperson for God and all that he does. That happens naturally. The gift was given, and it permeates everywhere in you and around you to others and even those of long distances away. They hear what you say and what you do, and are fascinated by your beliefs and ways that may have changed. It is what you do and say, and how you do it, that they find curious and want to learn more of what you have experienced. They seek it and find it in you.

You will see if you have been given this gift of light and love that you will be drawn to speak about it to others eventually, and they will take note of what you have experienced. They want it also. They want to feel what you feel. They want to be anointed with a gift so precious it changes them too. They want and seek it from you. So, do not be afraid of those who approach you and say I want what you want. I want to know what you know. I want to experience what you have experienced. They will come to it in their own time.

Be mindful that they are seeking the Lord and his ways also. They are on their journey to understand what they do not know or realize to be. They are wanting to walk in the light of the Lord also. You can see that we are all ready for a new beginning on Earth. It is your development process, and it takes some time to know when you are ready. It will come, and you will be ready and wanting at that time. You feel the need with the Lord. You seek the need in the Lord as he gives you what you ask for by his standards. He is all about giving you what you need and want according to his ways.

Many times people get something from the Lord, and they do not expand on the gift. They let it waste away to where they have no realization that they were given this gift. It sits there waiting to be used, and it is not used. That is laziness and profoundly irresponsible in the eyes of the Lord. You need to act on what is given you and react to the Lord's gift by using it freely and happily. Make others feel that you have a special trait or quality that enables you to be happy and joyous to others around you. This is the way of the Lord.

Spread the happiness to others. They need it as you can easily see in others when they speak to you about all their problems they are dealing with on Earth. Give the gift or use it in a way that helps someone. They will remember you and your gift always. You have helped someone by your nature and thought process to make someone see what you know and give it freely to others.

We see the response in others as they see the miracle you have inside of you. They witness you and what you are. They attend to your ways and see that all is different from them to you. You have something they want. So, give your gift freely, and make them aware of all that is good on the Earth. They will realize their gifts one day, and know what you have also. It is you giving yourself to others. They recognize what is special in you immediately after experiencing you as a person. Note you are reflecting God and his ways.

We carry our gifts with us, and we use them daily. We seek more gifts and want to know what others can do that we cannot do. We are all special in the eyes of the Lord. We all are his children and know his nature to be one and the same with ours. He has told it to be so. Let us then go, and use our gifts to help others in need. We have so much to give others that need our help. Let us expand our gifts and see what others have that we do not have. Let us also find those that are like us in nature and gifts and expand on them.

We see that you have so much to give others. So, let us begin anew to go forth, and help others daily. We are only as good as we can do for others. It is written that we are of nature with God, and so we must show it to others to be fulfilled in God's nature. Can it be more simple, or do I need to expound on this further?

Those that have not experienced this may one day experience it, but not everyone will. It is for those that have been chosen to receive this type of gift. There are many gifts that the Lord gives, and you can see it in them when you look upon them and their actions. Seek and look upon those, and see if you can see their gift(s).

Chapter 10

Curious in Nature Is Good

There are many disturbances in life, and we look for answers and where we can find them. We look to God, loved ones, Jesus, friends, and lovers to get an answer. Does it come? Sometimes the answers come to you, and sometimes it takes more time to consider what is happening around you. We know there are difficulties with everyone on Earth and see just what is happening to you. We can help in some ways but not in every instance. We are driven to help, but there are boundaries or limits that we face in order to do what is needed. It all depends on the person needing the help.

We see many that require help but cannot assist all because there are guidelines or rules we must follow. The person needs to be accepting of what we can give them. They have to know that we are from the Light of God and can see their problems and all they face in life. They must ask for help, and we can give what we can or are able to.

Many of us help in different ways. Some heal people. Some give advice first. Some carry another's burden. Some guide and direct. Some even take away burdens by extraordinary means. We do much to help, and you are not aware of all that we do for those in need. We are not visible to you, nor should we be. We are near you all the time. We can see you, but you cannot see us as we travel around you. We are present all the time.

Many of us have groups of helpers. We devise a plan to help. We consider our actions guided from God. He lets us know what we should be doing and why. We can alter a person's life in an instant by divine grace and power. We see all you do, and what you do not do. We have considerable power to be of assistance in many cases. More of us grow daily in numbers since we are called for specific measures. We are fortunate to have guides and mentors with us also. We learn as we go sometimes.

Many want us around all the time, but we cannot be there all the time based on the directions from God and other elders in spirit. We are taught to do what we do, and multiply our action through numbers. Normally, we are heard by those who need our words or communication. They hear us in their head or are prone to do another action based on our direction. We can influence people, and what they are doing to some degree.

We are spirit in nature and can fly or coast through the air with ease in different dimensions around the world and beyond. We are flightless since we have not wings to speak of. We are the energy you consist of. We are all helpers in a sense of a giving nature with divine province to correspond with. We act through the words of God, and we see the results of what we are trying to accomplish in someone. We help as seen fit to do with someone's problems and yearnings. All can be helped, but only through divine guidance.

Many behold that prayer is what we need to communicate with you, but that is not the case. We need a special communication and acceptance of that person to listen or hear us, and we hear them by their nature and gift they have been bestowed with. We see the light and act accordingly with others on Earth and beyond. More times we are accepting the problems you give us to help you with. We can do much and do often.

When there is no one to help you, we are there. When you hear no one around you, we are there. When you seem to hear or feel us around you, we are there. We can move to give you what you need at the time. There is not much lacking in what we can help with if shown the guidance from heaven and God and his essence. People seem to want instant relief, but that is not always possible. The guidelines are given to us for each person. Some may get help where others may not. Some have to live through a crisis to learn what they need to learn. We are guided by God in these matters of question and determination. We do not believe that we are helpless, just directed to individuals that we can see need our assistance.

There are many of us and help many even in one day; so many in one day that it is hard to count all of them. There are many requests for help even in the smallest of things that need mending. Life has a bit of turmoil in it all the time, and that is prevalent on Earth. There are so many needs to be met. We again cannot assist in all things, but help where we can.

Adequate time is needed by people to develop the skill of speaking with us. We are not on your wavelength, and this is vital to communicating with us. We can see what is normal to you and for you. We can see how we have to adjust your wavelength to correspond with ours. It is a gift that is given someone, and that is given freely by God. We know who can hear and listen to us and are fortunate to have someone that we can communicate with on Earth. This is lacking so more need to be given this gift of communication. It will happen in the near future, and we will be happy that it does.

Most people cannot even begin to understand how we communicate, and it is puzzling to them that we can speak to someone on Earth, but we can. It is done daily. These people with these gifts carry a burden to perform as needed, and they are not given much admiration for doing so. We tell you that it is a gift from God and he abides in that statement.

Much is to be done to help someone, and we can do it and are here to help in any way we can. We assure you that we do exist and are beside you many times throughout your day helping you as you go. Not much evades us since we know of all what is going on Earth. We accept your troubles as our own and problems to be solved. By our nature, we are helpers and can assist and be guided by your thoughts, deeds, and words.

We can locate you in an instant, and give you advice as needed. We can project our thoughts into yours. We can take action so critical it can save a life or stop something from happening. We have the power from God the Almighty on our side, and he has given us to assist you as needed and wanted.

Blessings on all of you as you go through your day. We are beside you and can assist you in your daily problems. We will be there for you in your time of need and prayer. Be mindful that we are just a moment away, and can be there for you in that instant.

Life can associate the world of people with so much energy, and we can fuel the energy even further with our thoughts and existence. We are not showing you all that we are, but are letting you know that we exist and can help you. No one can replace our nature since it is from God that we exist. He is our Lord and Savior also. We bow to him and are humbled by what he can do.

Life is a journey, so live and let live as you go forward in life on Earth. Be mindful of all that is around you. Your awareness is key to survival and insight. We bless and thank you. We are the angels of the Lord and are here for you. Not only do we speak his promises, we assure you that we assist him in his words to you.

Chapter 11

Take Heed
in the Way of the Lord

Temptations are around you all the time. We have remedies for all of these problems that come up and tempt you to do something that is unwise for you to do. We have thoughts, prayers, and suggestions that you can use to console yourself and others.

The first one is for tempting you to do no good or abhor to God. Sit back and close your eyes and think of God and his good nature. He will come to you and give you a resolution. Just ask him for a direction or what to do, and he will give you a suggestion or two for you to take. Relax in the Word of God for he is good and righteous.

There is something you can do if you are tempted to do evil in the eyes of the Lord; a quick prayer of asking God for to deliver you from this evil thought or idea. Evil is prominent on the Earth and elsewhere. You must act quickly before the evil enters you, and places its seed in you. You must remove it directly with the Word of God, and be mindful that you need to sit in the Word to relinquish the problem or the seed so as not to be set in you. God is the protector of all, and he can relinquish the evil from you in an instant. He who believes in me will be comforted, says the Lord, and that is so.

Much can be done if you are asking for forgiveness since you are forgiven in different ways by the Lord. He has forgiven your original sin and can forgive anything you ask of him. He is there listening to you when you ask. He can hear everything you say, think, and also do. God has a forgiving nature, and his Son bears that - was a witness to you.

If you are grieving over someone's death or misfortune, then you can go to God and ask all that you need. He is there to help with his goodness and character. He knows exactly what you need and why. He will give you what you need either instantly or in due time. There is no one who can comfort as the Lord, our God. He rejuvenates and makes whole the spirit, mind, and body of us all as needed. He is there for the asking. Ask, and you shall receive. He is always there for you.

When you are lonely, and you have no one, you still have God and all his angels and helpers there beside you. He is there comforting you in ways you do not know of. He knows your pain and gives you a lifting that no one else can give you in your time of need. God will not forsake you though at times you may think so. It is not true. It is his nature to help and be of assistance to you no matter where you are.

People will ask you for help, and you may not know how to give it. God will guide you in your endeavors to help someone that needs help. He is there, and so are many that can help in different ways. Be mindful that talking to God and others is a way of letting them know you are in need of help/assistance then and at the moment of despair. They can send help in an instant. You will feel the change or see the changes in people towards you. Help is always around. We can manipulate some things and relieve problems, so let us know what you need and why.

Much is done with people that have behavioral issues or problems. We watch them carefully and sense their limitations. We help in various ways by watching them and seeing their reactions to everything. Some of those people do not recognize God, and that is not necessary in order for us to help them. They have limited scope and awareness, and we know that, so we expand our help to them. They have trials in their life that are great and need some of our assistance. At times, they need comfort. We know what needs to be done to alleviate the problems people have. We are here to assist. Just tell us what you need, and we will have someone there to help you.

There are people who are in need from floods and storms. We can help them and direct them to where help is given. They need material things to get them by in their misfortune. We can do that to help them. We see many changes on the Earth and see vast amounts of water and storms. This is all part of God's plan, and we can send help and assistance to those who need the comforts to get them by in a crisis situation.

Many are asking for abundance, and this is given through God's grace. We cannot expect God's abundance all the time. We have to do what we are here on Earth to do and fulfill our purpose in life. He gives to those that he deems responsible to take care of that which is given. He knows where to plant his seeds that will flourish among you.

Life is given and so is death. All on Earth die eventually. It is a welcome change to many that seek the Lord. He waits for you in his kingdom/world, and he knows when you are due to enter heaven again to receive his Word and directions. Your developing soul is of great importance to him. He recognizes everyone and knows what to do with your needs and wants. He sees what you do and what you want or enjoy doing. Do not flounder, but be assured that he knows what you are and what you are doing. His directions and instructions are clear in your mind and body, so heed what you think and like. Be mindful not to overindulge in what you are given. Life is precious and should be lived with God in mind. His rules are meant to be obeyed or followed.

People whisper thoughts of indignation to others, and that is also heard. Your neighbor is like you and needs to be respected and honored as you would like to be honored and respected. People are just as you are. They have wants, needs, problems, difficulties, and mourn. So, be mindful of their needs as your own; like breeds like. Be faithful unto your brother, and he will respond back to you. Much work is to be done in this category since there is much confusion, dislike, hard feelings, bad thoughts, and so much rampant killing on Earth. Brothers are not noted as brothers, so there is much discontent between peoples. We understand and are working on these problems.

Much is given, and much is taken away. Needs of the many outweigh the needs of the few; it seems on Earth. The many are of a need so large that it is hard to fulfill. God sees the many as a large endeavor that needs help and assistance. We see all that is happening, and those forgotten souls need to be mindful of those who have what they do not have. We see that people just take and not give back. They steal and abduct where it is not their place or right to do. We relinquish their poverty yet they do not help themselves to be on their own and replenish what they have taken from others. This is not the way of the Lord. They must replace what is given to them either by deed or action through others. We see inconsistent behavior to many and do not want to adhere to God's laws or guidelines. There will be much to do with these people in God's kingdom. They lack compassion, forgiveness, and consideration to others who help them. Love is never-ending, and these people need to show love and understanding to those who have given them so much. God is great. God is good.

Generations to come will feel the Lord's words and deeds. He will flourish in many soon, and you will see his grace continue to help many on Earth. There is so much that he wants to accomplish on Earth, and you all will be a part of that action because through God all blessings flow. We see many good things and intentions on Earth, and they will happen as God said they would. Be a part of a Christlike journey, and you will flourish in God's nature. Much love to everyone that can see God's grace in all.

Chapter 12

Persistence in Your Goal

God is all around us in everything we do. There are spirits that at the command of our Lord can help you with your difficulties. We are here to help you in your endeavors. So, be mindful that we do exist and are around you by the command and will of God. He has not forsaken you in any way. He is there to help you, and when you realize that, you will know, that he is beside you in all things that you do and say to others. He helps you in your daily activities and is there to guide you in your decisions. He is about you all the time and can see what you do and hear what you say. It is his gift in power that you may be unaware of.

When you do or say something, it is his will that you get what you say you want. You will put out your asking, and you will receive it. It is your decision to receive it or reject it. You should evaluate it once it comes to you. Make a smart decision, since it is your decision that may alter your life considerably. You know that it will change your life but to what extent is probably the unknown at the time. Be very careful in your decision, words, thoughts, and inklings that you whisper inside of you. What you ask for or want, you will probably receive. It is a known quantity of nature that you get what you ask for.

It is the truth, and so be prepared to find that it may not be what you expected to receive in the first place. When you first think of something, you are wishing and hoping for the most delightful thing.

You think of it as almost perfect for you, but when it turns out to be something different and doesn't sit well with you, you want to reject it or give it away. This is normal. So, be careful what you wish for and be specific in nature, because you may get something, not to your liking or that has only a few attributes that you were thinking of, and you did not think it out very well in your head upon wishing for it.

We know the dilemmas you experience on Earth, and it appears that you are in a most unfortunate group of always wanting and needing something in your life. You ask for things that are made, and not peace of mind, happiness, or gratitude. You ask for riches, but do not seek the riches of heaven in your life. Which is more important to you? We know the answer is may God pour his blessings upon you and not all the riches of the Earth. His love and understanding in your troubled times is(are) worth more than a sack of potatoes or a bowl of rice. He shows you the way, and you will have what you need in life. His grace abounds. He is your sanctuary and keeper of your thoughts, wants, and desires. He will see that you get what you need to exist and be bountiful. So, seek the Lord and not the goods of the Earth while you are on Earth. All that you need will be given to you while you seek the Lord. It is rightfully so.

Many wish to be rich and prosper the way others do on Earth. They have purpose and are driven to do what they do. If it is acceptable to you, you can prosper in the Word of God. Hear him, and he will suit your needs to your liking. Do not despair in your misfortune, because that can change in an instant or short time. Life is too short to ignore all the wonderful things you have in Earth life. It is just for the asking and the taking. God will deliver what he promises to you.

God is not asking for you to constantly remind him of what you need. He knows what you need. He is aware of your needs and wants always. He sees what you need and what you do to get what you need. He is there beside you in your home and walking beside you. There is no other like him that is all knowing and comforting. He wants you to succeed in being happy and purposeful with your life. He is waiting to see all the good you will do in your life. He sees it all, good and bad, harmonious and distasteful to him. He watches and waits for you to do what you were meant to do on Earth.

He can often remind you what you were supposed to be doing or working on in your life. He is there prompting you to get busy and do your life's purpose. He knows there are many distractions on the Earth, and it is up to you to focus on your life's purpose and get busy doing what you need to work on in conjunction with him. He is willing to wait to see you progress in the tasks at hand. He will decide your next changes and education, so that you may be lifted in his presence.

God is good in nature and wants you to abide by his laws and guidelines. He wishes that you take comfort in his presence, and be mindful of his yearnings towards you. He wants you to do well. He wants you to be successful in your goals and aspirations. He admits to being sometimes anxious for your success and is there reminding you to go ahead, do not be afraid or nervous because I am with you. He is there. You have to understand that yes, he is there for you. You may not see him. You may not hear him, but he is there in all that you do and say. He is there awaiting your act of kindness, or your decision. He is there giving a helping voice or hand in the matter.

Your life purpose is what you need to accomplish in your life - this life. He knows all the difficulties on your path and is relieving some of the burdens you face, but you speak to him and ask him for his help and guidance. He will not just give it without a request either by you or someone who knows you. He is wanting a personal relationship with you, and if you abide, he will answer.

Much work is involved with one life. There are so many beings that are around you daily with all that you do and wherever you go. They are there to assist you in your time of need, whether that need be a question, decision, or opinion. We are there to help and assist as we have already said. I do not think you can imagine how many are helping just one person daily. You would be astounded to find out who and how many are helping you. You do not realize all that is being done in your favor. You cannot count the number of beings helping all those people on the Earth. It is an unmistakable number that is only for us to know at the moment. We are here helping many. We are not just working with you but with many at the same time.

We are your advisors and seekers of the truth to help and guide you in whatever you are doing. We know you do not realize all that we do for you, but that is our existence and duty to the Lord our God. We are happy to assist and be counted; a true nature with God the Almighty. We are taskmasters and are more than pleased to help in your associations and countless questions. We are here to serve by the hand of God, and it shall be so for now and forever.

Chapter 13

What Misfortunes
Do You Encounter?

Time will tell your usefulness with the Lord. God is watching and waiting for you to come unto him and ask or tell him your wishes to do work under his guidance. He knows that you want to help with his work on the Earth if you tell him so. It is up to you to declare your interest in doing what you can for him and his cause on the Earth. He wants you to declare and be able to perform those duties he sets forth upon you. He must know that you want to do what he has for you to do. You may not be ready. You may not be willing at that time. You may be busy with many other things, and do not have the time to give to our Lord and Savior. He is patient and can wait. Though, when you are ready, you must declare it to him. He knows that there are many things going on in your life on Earth, and it is sometimes hard to fit into your busy schedule what you want to do for him. He knows all that and more. He wants the intent to be done, so that you will make some time for him and what he has for you to do.

Life brings upon many responsibilities, and you must take care of others, your duties to your work, and household. It is your decision to come to the Lord, and ask for his help in what you do. It is more work on your part to declare your interest in helping the Lord, and what he has for you and others to do on Earth. Life abounds no matter your decision, and it may not be the right time for you to do so or more for the Lord. He knows all of that and sees what you are doing daily. It is no secret to him. He asks that you be sincere and eager to help. He appreciates your mindfulness and sincerity.

We are many that do his work daily, and it is of your nature to want to do so also. We see that you are so conscientious in your work. He knows you are a persistent, good worker in things you like to do. He sees you hard at work in whatever you choose to do on Earth. Careful consideration is required on your part to make the correct decision, and when that time is near you need to declare it to the Lord, so he hears your wish and desire. He will use you for good and a just cause. Many work for him currently, and are all busy with what he has wanted us to do for him. It is a continuous need on the Earth.

Many people want to tune into what God wants. Many are eager to hear God's words. This work is not a passive undertaking. It requires more than just sitting in a Church praying. It is actual work that requires more time and effort. It takes time and commitment to others, with others, or for others. It is for the good of mankind that God wishes this work to be done. He is always looking for people to do, create, witness, respond, speak for him, or do some type of important work, that he requires or sees the need to be done. We all need help, and this is only one way that God seeks to help by using other people to transmit or transpond his thoughts or endeavors to others. He is waiting patiently for you to respond to what you will do for him.

You see how some people are so committed to their work for the Lord, and he relishes in the fact that you are working so hard for his cause on Earth. He is in deep prayer that you will succeed in what you are willing and attempting to do for him. He will help you accomplish what you set out to do in that what he wants you to do. He is with you always. So, do not be hesitant that you will not succeed. You will at some point in time. He is there to help so that one day you will have that task accomplished, and he will relish in the fact that you have completed your part of the whole endeavor. You are one in many that will work for the Lord. It is so, and it will be so. Be unto the Lord, and he will show you the way.

Many start a task and find it difficult, but eventually, it does get done with God's help and guidance. There are many others to help you in this task. It will be easier than you might think at first. We are always around you to help with what you want to accomplish in life. The Lord is willing and most able to help anyone with anything that they are trying to do. It is his nature to help as needed. He knows what you are experiencing, feeling, saying, and he knows what you need. Eventually, if you recognize what you need and say it unto him, he will hear you and respond in some way. He sees the problems you are facing, and it is with his great pleasure to help you in all things. Just speak to him, and he will answer.

Life may appear hard, and it wears you down to where you feel you cannot accomplish even the small tasks that are upon you, but you can. It just takes a little more time, patience, and persistence to do what you set out to do. Time to do what is needed is one of your daily tasks. This would be added to your list of what I need to do today. Sometimes, the work for him gets put off to another day, and that is when God is patiently waiting. Do not be hard on yourself, because he knows what all you have to do in your daily routine. He knows all that need your help in what you are trying to accomplish. He waits and reminds those that need reminding that he is waiting patiently, and wants or needs you to accomplish your set of tasks for him.

Much is given to those who walk with the Lord. He is great, and he is good. Be aware that you would be doing God's work, and he will know that it is being done by you and others. It is for a good and just cause. From the smallest of tasks to the most difficult, he recognizes what you are doing and how well you do it. He sees the many attempts you have done in your life to follow him with your actions, and he is pleased that your nature is of a godlike fashion. You are his feet, hands, minds on the Earth, and he helps you in your endeavors and wants you to succeed no matter how small or large the task. God is great. God is good. He is your Redeemer and Savior. God watches over you and wants you to do well. He recognizes everything that you are doing for him. God bless you in your efforts.

There is much to accomplish, so do not sit idle too long. Jump into action for the time is passing, and much is to be done for others. He is awaiting your words and would be pleased to see you flourish in your efforts. Be still and aware that he is there with you; next to you in all you do. God will never forsake you or leave you. He is the Holy Lord of Mankind.

Chapter 14

Make Haste in
What You Want to Do

Many people look to the Lord for favor, but it is not a reason to do good works for the Lord. Good works are from your inner soul. It is what you want to accomplish, that makes you who you are as a being. For many, that is their life's work. They always do for others, but others find it difficult to work for others or do for others. This is a challenge, and it makes you feel odd at first doing this type of work. Well, it is for your benefit to help others, and they shall, in turn, help you. If not them, then someone will. That is how life is on Earth. It is a help one another type of existence. We, too, do unto others as is his will also. This is a divine nature.

You can ask someone to help, and they reject the idea, while others will jump to help. That is their nature that is showing in a time of need. Not everyone is willing to help. Their tasks are more important to them, and they may think that someone will help instead. That may be true, but you were in that place and time, and you were called upon, but yet you did not help. You were not available to another who needed your help. I know if you needed help, you would want someone to help you in your space and time. It is just how life is on Earth.

There is a great need, and it should or must be fulfilled. People are learning, and experiencing new things as their development increases and changes. They need certain things from other individuals, and they ask for help. They seek out help in different ways. It is for some to step forward with that help, and for others, it is their task to be onto the next thing that needs to be done. We are all trying to get what we need to (be) accomplished, but there is always some time to help one another as you go on your path. This is the way of the Lord.

Much is to be done, and more so now. We are entering a time of great turmoil, and people will need much. They will have less and less. They will require more to sustain themselves in certain locations. It is a need that we need to fulfill as we can. The Earth is changing, and it needs to be transitioned and cleansed. It is a task only God can do. If you think about the vastness of that task, you will see no one else could do it.

He requires that you become aware of the changes in the environment and move to safekeeping. He is aware of those who linger but should leave a location. It is/was their choice. God wants you to be safe and enjoy life. Life will always change, and we need to be ready to move if needed. Turmoil is change in a haphazard way. It is the result of those not listening, or have let their awareness reduce to nothing. It is only a short time, and the calamity is over. Then, your life has changed, and it is on another track - more to do in a different way possibly.

Your life is transitioning. You are transitioning. Everyone is transitioning. You can see that there is constant change all around you, and we all need help in those changes in some way. One should accept help joyfully if it is pertinent to the problem. If you know of the right way or of the solution, you should help and be happy to do so. Others will appreciate your help if you know what you are talking about. Character is important.

Never expect something for your help. Give it freely; a few words, a suggestion, or possibly even a long explanation of what needs to be done. It is your chance to do something more than words also - a helping hand or some time to help with another's project. It is all good since both or whoever is involved will gain some happiness in helping one another. It is the way of the Lord. So, be cheerful and eager to help with someone's problem/dilemma.

These acts of kindness need time to accomplish, so scheduling your time is important. Be mindful of your time and other duties, so that you do not slight others. We know that you want to accomplish so much, and this is another way of allowing others to accomplish what they need to do also. It is a good and honorable thing one does to help another. Go with God and love the Lord for he is good.

Chapter 15

Collaborate with All around You

Your life can be determined by two things - acceptance and knowledge. These are two very important to accomplish in your lifetime. Many strive to know more and gain as much knowledge as possible, and this is a wise thing to do. With more knowledge then you have much to contribute to others. You gain self-worth and are harmonious in knowing what you know. It is a great gift to have knowledge and use it to benefit others.

Acceptance is another quality that is favored because it allows one to see past their own limitations. They can open their mind to new and interesting ways, ideas, creations, words of thought, and get past the restrictions we place upon ourselves. This is a remarkable gift that leads to more knowledge and gifts bestowed upon oneself. With this insight into the unknown you can see wondrous possibilities, and experience such that you have never done before. It is the key to understanding, further knowledge, new viewpoints and a way different from your way of looking at the world, and what is all about the world and beyond.

Much can be deciphered from opening your old ways into a new way, seeing what is not familiar and looking for the unknown. It is a journey and interesting, to say the least. We see that you hunger for knowledge and exploration. We see you want to know and experience more. Well, here is the chance.

Acceptance means a number of things in your life; acceptance of others, acceptance of who you really are, acceptance of your faults and capabilities, acceptance of those around you for who they really are, acceptance of your true life and purpose on Earth and beyond, and acceptance of the nature of the world and what it has in it, acceptance of what another has to exchange with you whether that be hospitality, love, words, ideas, suggestions, another viewpoint on ways to do and experience, and so much more. Acceptance covers so many things, and it is a wondrous journey at times to experience it all.

If you accept your misgivings, faults, errors, lack of, susceptibilities, nature, and go deep within yourself to find your true self and nature, it will lead you to your purpose. It will lead you to understanding of who you are in the world and how you are with others. It will lead you to what you know you can do, and what others will need to help you with. You are of a true nature, and you will find out what that is when you accept all that you are or are not.

This process takes time and deep thought of yourself, your actions, your problems that you experienced and more. You can see that to know one's self is to honor your presence and to eventually acknowledge your purpose in this life. We see much done in self-awareness, and this is good for the being or soul. It humbles you in knowing your limitations and capabilities. One can always gain knowledge and with this more understanding of the world and the Universe. It is helpful to gain as much knowledge as you can, and take that with you on your journey.

Self-development is important in your life. It is the key to more opportunities for you to do more with and for others. It is a basic need that needs to be fulfilled. We only see ourselves for a long time during our growth, but then there is a time that we need to go beyond that and see what others see, feel, do, and think. We are creatures of exploration, research, understanding, possibilities, and want to go further along in our journey. Each small accomplishment adds to the whole of what you have or are doing. Each small gesture to another adds to the whole of your love to another and self.

We see it all, and it is good when you extend yourself beyond what you are at that moment in time. We see you becoming more whole in nature; more balanced as a true creature of God. We see you expanding and developing as you progress in your life. We see that it is good and you develop with reflection and awareness of yourself and others. It is the way you should be developing. Do not ignore yourself, your wants and needs, since they are what you need to move forward in your life and beyond.

Life is a precious thing, and you are experiencing it firsthand. You are witnessing difficulties. You are experiencing more than most over lifetimes of trial and error it seems. You will, eventually, find your way to the best you can possibly be, and that is through your words, actions, deeds which are closer to godlike. You will know it when you get closer to God from your actions and faults. You will know when you have been redeemed of your past problems and disabilities. You will know it when you are onto a brighter path unto God.

You will know it when you have reached a true peak into a transition that brings you more joy and love with God. You will know it when you have done all you can, and there is no one else to surrender to but God. You will it when you can say I did what I could, and now I give it all to God for him to handle for his is the Lord of all and knows how to handle it all without me doing anything more. You can surrender it joyfully since God will take care of it all. He is our Lord and Redeemer and oversees us. He is our caretaker. He is our Father in heaven. He sees, knows, and loves all. Be blessed that you recognize him and all he does for you and everyone. Lord, grant us your blessings on Earth and in heaven. God is good, and he will reign forever and ever. There is no doubt about this.

We accept our role and work with the Lord, and so should you to be one with the Lord our God. We have duties to perform. We guide, help, teach, explain, perform acts of goodness, and more. We accept our role with God, and so should you. It is a wonderful journey, and we begin to tell you how wondrous it all is. We accept great pleasure on pleasing God. We shine with glee and joy when we accomplish what we need to do for him.

We are certain you will experience that also. It is forthcoming to you if you accept what God has in store for you given your true nature and acceptance of him as your Lord and Savior. He adorns and blesses you on your path of living, accepting, and doing the work of the Lord. Peace be with you now and forever.

Chapter 16

Commemorate Your Love to Others

To all who want to visit the extrasensory world, we are here to guide you into the real of love and consciousness. We are here to help you in any way we can. There is a notion that we are not real, or we are mistaken for other beings. Well, this is not so. We are real, worthy of existence, and at will to do God's work everywhere we are called to participate. There is much to be done here and elsewhere that we are quite busy doing our duties for others.

You can contact us with your word, and we will be at hand for you. You can wish it, and it will be so. You can dream it, and it can come to fruition. You can make believe that it can happen, and it will. You can do all that and more, and it will be unto you, and we are here to help make it all happen. We guide and seek guidance. We love and seek love. We train and are trained by others. We adorn and are loved, and adorned by others. We know no limits and create none in ourselves and others. We see the path and take it joyfully. We notice all that is good and reasonable in a person and being. We judge not and are not judged by those in a higher power. We are here to help you along your way to a higher consciousness.

Seek us, and you shall find us. The same is with the Lord. We are ever present in life, love, and nature. No one can say we do not exist, and be aware of our presence. We can overpower your illnesses, doubts, speculations, and make them disappear in a moment. We are all abiding in the Lord who gives us strength. No one can take our gifts from us since they are given from the Lord and bestowed upon us with love and duty. Acceptance is ours to give. We make it so, and so it is, just as the Lord has spoken to us.

No one can hinder giving except a rejection from a soul, who does not want to receive what we offer. In many times we give it so freely, it is accepted and not rejected. It is good to be accepted for your gifts and good deeds to another. You know how it makes you feel when you give, and it is accepted by another. It is the same for us. We love doing what we are doing. We cannot control where we are sent but are more than willing to go as directed or called.

We see the Light of God in many, and they use their gifts wisely and properly. We ask that you do the same. We are here to make your life better, and more liking to your soul. Not all can witness these gifts since they are dealing with other problems/troubles that have to be worked through before they can realize more of what is happening around them. They have their own path to undertake, and it is their task at hand that is of importance to them.

Much is given, and much is retained by many. We give love and make things happen to allow the occurrence to be available. We give wisdom, and show the truth from the Light of God. We give caring and healing as needed. We give our gifts that we harbor in our being/soul, and hope you share the feelings and longings to give as we give unto you.

It is truly a wondrous feeling when you receive a gift, and your life and perspective changes. The Universe rejoices when you are bestowed a gift and begin to use it wisely for others, and your changes are relevant to what you are doing or experiencing. It is truly amazing many times the feelings of rejuvenation, and restoration that one feels. It changes your life and existence. It nurtures your soul, and you know that we are present in your life. You know you have been changed. The lost hope is gone. The emptiness is gone, and your heart is full again. Your loss is taken away, and you have regained your heart back as a whole. Much is given, and much is taken and given away. We see this and are pleased that you follow the Lord and his ways of doing what is meant to be done.

Caring is what we need to do and is asking for favor in times of trouble. Ask, and it shall be given. You know this and are needed to be reminded of that statement. It is true. You need to ask God for what you think you need, and he will give it and even more at times. Your restoration is important to him, for you need his rejuvenation in your life. He sees it. He knows it. He bestows it on you, and you barely recognize that it was given from him. He has done you great favors and blessings in your life. It is time to recognize all that he has done for you.

Think back to when you were small and knew nothing of the Earth and all that is has in it; this of the things you enjoyed, favored, and could not get enough of. Think of all that you disliked, abhorred, and found distasteful. Think of what you lacked, and what you had. It was all a plan or journey for your soul to take and grow from. It is this journey that is for you to understand and connect with.

There is purpose in all that you do, say, and discover. There is purpose in the way you conduct yourself with others, and what you do in life that matters. There is a reason why you are here doing what you are doing every day. There is no lack of reason. There is no lack of purpose. Just, maybe, you do not know what it is in your life. This is where self-awareness, meditation, preservation of the soul through righteous acts, planning the next good thing you are going to do for another, and so forth till the end of your days in this lifetime. You are here for a reason, and it is your efforts to seek out what your true purpose is and true nature of your soul. That is why you are seeking your awareness in life, your life, your existence, and where it will take you.

There is not lack of judgment with people, and that is a profound mistake. We are all working our way through life's problems and struggles. We are all seeking favor from the Lord. We may not know how to get there, or what to do, but we are struggling and trying our best, so we think. There is more here that needs to be said. Life is a concoction of calamities, and it is one of our purposes to not get caught up in the mix of confusion and dire need. We must step back, look at what we need to do, pray and ask for help, sometimes step back and let God handle the most difficult of situations since he knows and does all for others, and sometimes just let it be and see what happens, so we can just let it be with us. Maybe now is not the time to figure it out, but recognize it, and say it will be dealt with later.

Time is short on the Earth, and we all know that it would be good to do good while we are present on the Earth with so many people struggling to do better in their lives and feel connected to others and a higher being. They need proof but do not recognize it in their lives daily. They need more insight into their own lives. They need to think about what has transpired in their lives up to that time.

Look back on all that you have done, remembered, interacted with others in your life. What hardships did you overcome? What did you learn? What did you seek? What did you long for? What did you ask for, and it was not given at the time? There are so many questions to answer yourself. What have you attained, and is it what you really need to attain, or is there more to do? What can you say about yourself that others have not witnessed yet? What have you known for so long about yourself but have not used? What is it that spurs you on to do more and more without reservation? We know, but you have to know to take the next steps and deliver yourself to the hands of God, where he will make you whole and meaningful again and again. He is your Restorer and Redeemer. There is no lack in you as an individual.

All people are working on what they need to work on. All people are finding challenges and tasks that need to be fulfilled or completed. These are your tasks that you have given to yourself from above before you were here. You know what you want to do in a situation. You know what it is you are probably working on in yourself and with regard to others. You know because it was your decision to work on it.

We honor your work and give help to you wholeheartedly as you need it. All you have to do is ask. God speaks your praises on all good that you do. He rejoices in your accomplishments and sees the good that you do. He does not contain himself. He is right there with you when you are given such joy. He is there and others along with him who rejoice in your favor. There is no holding back his delight upon your completing a task or purpose that is within you. He sees it, recognizes it, and is there to honor your work. Much is given, and much is received.

So, carry your honorable work within you, and be proud of all that you do - be it right and just. Do not falter and give up, but proceed to work on and accomplish what you set out to do. If a task is half done, then consider the time when you will return to finish it and do it as well as before. Finish it with delight and pleasure, that it was a job well done and with good intent. Be happy and rejoice in all your accomplishments no matter how small for in the eyes of the Lord it is a well-mastered task.

It is good to bestow your knowledge on others, so they can feel the goodness of completing a task also. They will work hard and long just to do what you have accomplished. Love abounds with others in need of the same thing or of what you have. You can feel the presence of all that want to experience what you experience in this world and others if that was your experience. We all need to know what others know and experience, so we keep our connection. We all want to be connected in the sight of the Lord. It is so, and it is done.

Chapter 17

Disturbance Is Negligible

There is a light in everyone that shines through to the outside of the body, and it is your aura. It emanates all that you are on the inside; who you are and what you are feeling. It is noticeable to only a few that see you when you walk by them. It is a means of identification to some, and a warning to others. Some can see your focus in life by visualizing the colors. Each color has a meaning. It is your job to know what these colors mean and visualize them coming from another person. This is a good indication that they are well or in need of help in some way.

We see your colors and adjust them and you occasionally. We see that many need help, and we assist them as they go throughout their life. We see that you are open to others, willing to help, trying to do something difficult, in sorrow, or bad times. We see it all and accommodate you in various ways so that your burden is not so problematic.

No one can know all the spectrum of colors down on the Earth since you can see all types of shading and vibrancy that is possible. We show you what you can see, and what you cannot is left to your imagination. We have a vast spectrum of colors that we can see. We gaze at all the beauty and dwell in its colors and frequencies. It is good for the soul to be able to witness all that God has created for everyone to see. We know that your change of colors is significant to your body and mind. We hope that you can minimize your problems with therapy and adjustments in your color spectrum within your body. It is healthy to do so.

Not everyone can see these colors, and they are not meant for everyone to see at times. There is a limitation to viewing all the many colors upon the Earth. There is a vibrancy that we see only in the heavens that are not like any other. Much work is done with light and color. It is good to use colors and see as many colors as you can. It makes your view of the world better. It picks up your frequency and then distributes it among others you are near. It is a good thing to focus on colors and light among yourselves. We see much work is needed to be done with light and colors still. Not many people use them for therapy or health circumstance, but it does help with one's nature and disposition.

We can see colors among many when we look at them. We can see their various colors as we speak to them and know that they are changing in their thinking, knowing, and disposition. It is a joy to see someone change for the better, and know that they are on their way to healing or better health. We can see much change in people, and much change is needed. We see the dangers in the darkness of others. We see that they need tuning and frequency changes, but it is not all up to us to change them. They need to work on themselves also. They need to know that they need to improve and make adjustments in their life and thinking.

People are brought on the Earth to grow, learn, and witness others. People need to be diligent in what their purpose on Earth is, and be well in doing that. Changes occur over time, and that is reasonable when there is so much to be done. We look for change in who we help. We look for multiple changes in various colors to know that we and they are on the right track in healing and restoration. We are pleased when major changes occur for the better, and life is good again for that person. We see many changes, and it requires time to heal and grow within also. We see over time what most cannot see since we are a part of the changes that are experienced by those on Earth and beyond. We see good changes to those that persist in the way of the

Lord and want to change for the better and work at it. These changes are sometimes permanent changes, and they are restorative in nature. We hope you desire change for the good in the years to come and be with God and his nature. He is good, and he is great.

Many want to change but require our assistance. We see the struggle and are aware of your problems. We see all those that are hindering your good growth. We are assured, that you are trying to move in the proper direction but have fault or have fallen back to a disintegrating nature. We help you push forward with a boost of helpful energy and then other things we may do to help. We see you attempt to do better but have some problems in doing so. We are here to help and guide you. We are assured that you are put on the right track again and sometimes again and again. We persevere as you do in trying or attempting to get better.

We are sometimes in the form of light. We are energy and can be various forms. We are truly energy that is changing to allow for others to witness our performance and duties. We see that you are an ever-changing being and want to better yourself. We see that you are without cause to not want to better yourself. We know this and work with you daily. We see your struggles, development, many challenges, sorrows, disappointments, and finally success in your accomplishments. It is a fine thing to witness someone that is achieving a step closer to purity and righteousness. It shows your hard work is blooming in the sight of God and others.

We see you daily and know that you are trying and attempting to be better in all you do. Life is hard and not so easy with so many responsibilities to achieve under such difficult circumstances. You have many challenges daily in your life on Earth. We see all that you do and say. We hear all that you think and avoid saying to others. We listen and are aware of your desires and needs. We are here to help you and be your helper in time of need. We give glory to God and obey his words. We are living in a time frame not known to you. We are here and will be here for your needs to be met, and we offer assistance as best we can do for you. We are always around and can help. Be alert to our whimsies and pleasantries. We are all about and can help as was said already.

Much is to be done to improve your ways, and we are here to assist you. We want you to not look back to the old ways that were wrong in nature. Loving is a kindness we cannot take away from someone. It is their duty to issue love to another. We see that strife is from so many problems, but love is not one of them. Love is your kindness, consideration, happy thoughts, yearning to be with someone, doing for another who needs help, and so much more.

We see the need for love in all phases of love. We see it needs to be exploded on the Earth with it flowing in all directions. It would be a burst of energy to share with everyone. Love is in the air, and you breathe it in like oxygen. That would be the best remedy for the Earth at this time, but we rely on you to all do your part, and share your love with others to make it grow and abound within all creatures. We see a great need, and it is relevant to what you can do as a being on the Earth.

Everyone needs the love and tenderness of caring bestowed upon them. It is your function or job to do what you can to relieve other people's suffering or neediness there on the Earth. We see so much want and disaster that it requires you to do something to alleviate the problems there. We see that you know of all these problems, and yet do nothing at times. We need you to be more generous with your time and giving of yourself to help alleviate all that you do not like to see in others and yourself.

Love is a boundless energy. It moves and grows throughout time and space. We need you to do your part in helping others on the Earth. We see it and say to you again - we need you to help in this restoration NOW. There is no more time allowed to not do what you need to do to help another person or creature.

Time is calling out, that there is no more time. We need to restore what was lost. We need to jump in with both feet and hands and do something to restore the love and grace God has given each and every one of you on Earth. The time is NOW, and it is to be done. God has spoken. He wants it so. He sees some good going on, but it is not enough to overcome all the hurt and dissatisfaction with the world today.

So, step into the problem and make it your own, and alleviate the stress and needs of another by helping and giving of yourself to another. Do it wholeheartedly, and God will see that it is being done to your benefit and the world's benefit. Be not hesitant in doing what needs to be done. You will know what needs to be done because we will help you with your endeavors along the way. We see all that needs help and can assist in some way or another.

Do not think it cannot be done because it can and will be done. It is a monumental task, and it is a start to just want, but you need to give and do to make it so. We see that you are hesitant. Do not be so. Be aggressive in your determination to achieve what needs to be achieved. We will help and will continue to help even if you get tired and weary of the task. We see it and can help, and will help all those that need assistance. Do not worry, or fear anything that is new or abhorrent in nature. This needs more attention and help since it has fallen into disaster in nature. It needs caring and growth in the right direction to survive and flourish. We can help again and again. We can help restore the forgotten in nature. We have capabilities to help as you go along your path. Be not afraid for we are with you helping and aiding in the process of restoration and growth. We are your guides and angels keeping you on the path of restoration and glory in God's eyes. Be mindful that good is great in the eyes of the Lord.

No one will flounder. No one will be lost because your goodness will flourish in and among others. Nothing is lost in doing good to one another. Not one ounce of goodness is lost in the world. It is all for the betterment of mankind and creatures that abound with you. All creatures we say. No one can diminish love and its goodness.

We are here to help make it so for you and others. We see all goodness flowing into the depths of your soul and wanting to be given to another. This is good to see, and it is revealing that you are ready to give unto others as they would have given unto you. It is the way of the Lord, and it is so. Be mindful in your journey and do not forsake the goodness in you. It is always there to give unto another. God bless and keep you in God's spirit and nature. Behold he is upon you and giving you his life force within you to use and make well.

Chapter 18

Life on Earth Is Short

Man is upholding certain beliefs that are not to his liking. He believes in many things that are not so to be true. Man(/Woman) does not know the way to the truth, but yet it is there for all who seek the truth. Man believes in religion, yet no religion is a true total reflection of what God has intended for us. People state opinions and ignore the facts. People say this is so and that yet do not prove it to be so. People say one thing and say another later on. People are so confused to the true nature and will of God the Father. He is not all what you think of him. He is a true spirit of true nature to all that exist(s).

God will tell you what you need to know of him, and he seeks your understanding of him and his Kingdom in heaven. He is of divine nature and is like no other that you have known before. He is and always will be, and that is a fact and a truth. He is of higher will and destined to be Ruler of All by his Word and your deed to his bountiful nature.

We see that you flounder and do not really know the truths that rule your Earth. The laws are not clear to you. We see you trying to figure out what should be done. Is this right? Is that right? No one says right or wrong at times, and you still flounder to know what is truly right and wrong. We have laws under God, and they are to be respected and followed. By his law, we are redeemed and judged. It is his will and nature you are dealing with; no one else.

We see that his Word is sometimes spoken foreign to you in that you cannot figure it all out. There are interpreters on Earth to help you decipher all that is written. There are knowledgeable people that know what the trueness of God's nature and Word is. He sees to it that the Word is upon you if you need it. He speaks in your favor and wants you to hear what he has to say.

He knows everything about you and knows what you are dealing with on the Earth. He knows you inside and out. He knows what you seek, want to learn, want to do, and how to be recognized by others (and) in how you are in communication and personality. He sees you for who you are and understands like no other. So, be willing to go to him, seek him out, talk to him, know his words, know who he is in nature, and want to follow him with the others that follow him. He is waiting for all to follow him and be right with the Lord. He does not seek to hurt or hinder you at all. He is your friend, Redeemer, Father in heaven, and is of good and kind nature. You need to seek him and say his words out loud for others to hear.

He waits to hear the voices from Earth shouting his name, and saying God in heaven we come to you and ask for your true words of healing and restoration. We are in need of your help, and want your hand to be placed on us so that we may recover from all that is not Christlike in nature. We are here to surrender to you, Lord of All. We are here to listen to your words and act upon them. We are your followers and are here to help in any way we can. He is waiting for those words to sound out from your mouth/lips. He is here and everywhere listening for your words to exemplify your true nature and understanding purpose on the Earth. He knows you will come to him eventually, but it is a good time NOW to come to him, and be one with him and him alone in Spirit.

You can do all this and more under God's influence. You can learn so much through the Word of God that it is to your benefit to do so. You can be like an apostle of Christ on the Earth, even today with all that is going on in the world. So many have tried and not done what you are trying to accomplish. Let God help you as you go along. This is one thing that is a surety in your life. God is there waiting to help you. Just say what you want out loud to him, and he will respond. Speak of your misgivings, frailties, loss, desperation, sickness, greed, disrespect of others, lack of understanding, and much more to him, and he will show you the way under his hand and guidance. God is will in thoughts and endeavors that only God shall teach you the ways of the Lord. Seek, and thee shall find in the name of the Lord. Amen.

So much awaits you that you cannot begin to fathom the enormity of it all. You will have vast, enormous feelings of joy and loving the way it makes you feel. You will have wisdom and other graces bestowed upon you while you follow him in his ways and laws. He will reveal them to you in different ways. There is no other like him anywhere. He knows that you want answers. He knows that you want healing and forgiveness of your misdeeds. He knows that you seek knowledge and understanding. He will give it to you. Just ask for it. He will give it to you.

There are many who ponder religion and look into the intricacies of one or many religions hoping to find the real answers. Hoping is not doing or experiencing the words and the truth. Do unto others as they would do unto you. Do not hope. Do not wish upon a star. Do not flounder in despair. Keep doing. Keep searching. Keep talking to God. Keep aligning yourself with the Word of God, and he will reveal himself to you. We tell you to fix yourself upon the Word of God. Study and understand the Word of God.

If you cannot, then rely on someone to tell you the Word of God. Let them tell it to you, and wallow in the Word until it is a part of you. There are many learned individuals on the Earth that have a good understanding of the Word that you seek that will offer you peace and truth. There is all what you need. You are all that you need since many capabilities are within you to understand the words that God gives you. He is pure and righteous. You can follow him with no discourse, but you must understand him fully and not just think you understand him and his words. Look to the scriptures to understand Jesus and his nature. Look to the one that understands the Lord best. There are some great orators on the Earth, and they have some answers for you to follow and be happier in the Word of God and your understanding of him.

Praise God for his goodness and deeds, his blessings, and recognize all that he has done for you. He has given you graces, blessings, knowledge, peace of mind, healing, rest in his Word, patience, kindness, traits to deal with others, and so much more. He is your Father that gives you life and breath. Use what he has given you wisely. Become what your spirit is telling you to become. Be honest with yourself to find your true nature and purpose. Act upon what it is God wants you to do. He gives you hints and reminders in various ways so that you will stay on your path of your purpose on Earth. He has given you the body and feet to walk upon the Earth, so do so with dignity and honor and respectfulness.

You are like him, so be like him and follow him and his words. He knows that you strive to be better and grow within yourself, but to what end? What is your purpose on Earth, and are you fulfilling it? Are you working to be better, more open, more responding, more helpful, more caring, and stay within that mindset, so you can continue to be that way once you have found your purpose and destiny that is yours alone to fulfill?

We are in a time that is a time for standing our ground with God by our side. We are at a time when we should reflect on God's words, and shout them to others for them to understand and be in his glory also. We are at a time when God wants our awareness focused on replicating good in the world even by laws and restrictions. There is rightfulness in limiting what others do to others. There is a good and a not so good way to relate to others. There is stability in following out the Word of the Lord.

God wants followers and doers under him. He wants those that seek him and shout his name in reverence and respect. He is the one who made us and is aware of us always. He is not to be forgotten in anything we do or say. We are told to be unto the Lord for he is good and holy. The Lord will seek you out at times and give you more than what you ask for. Watch, listen and understand what he is doing for, with, and within you. The mysteries of the Earth will unfold more and more, so be witness to God and his work with you. Be unto the Lord for he is good. Amen.

Chapter 19

Command Your Life and Take Hold of It

It is of man's(/woman's) nature to be honored and respected by others, but man needs to stand for the righteousness of God the Father in what he does or does not do. He needs to know that he is doing the right thing when it comes to following the Word of God. He must seek this within himself, and God will speak to him, and let him know what the right thing to do in many cases is.

People always do not follow what they are to do but follow along with others. They ignore the signs and the teachings of the Lord. They just go and do what seems to be fun at the moment, or what others think is the right thing to do, but it is not so many times. People ignore God's true words and take his Word, rearrange it into something they can live with and not what God says you should live with. He has laws, and many do not know his laws or seek them out. God will explain them to you; just ask. If you do not hear him for some reason, seek out the answers in other ways. The answers will come to you in one way or another.

It is a time of renewal for the Earth. It is a time of standing on and with the Word of God. It is a time to be joyous, that the true nature of God is upon you today. So, be present in this gift he gives you and respond in like and kindness to others. This gift is a precious peace for the Earth. He thinks a restoration is needed to align everyone more to God and the ways of God. Replenish and restore. Be mindful of what goodness there is on the Earth and do it in your ways or your abilities to give back to others and the Earth. Your wisdom is needed to help with the restoration of the planet and all that is. Your help is needed to help with the mindfulness and taking care of others. Your help is needed to revitalize all that you see and do. You are the children of God. You are his keepers of the Earth. You are his witnesses to his Word and deeds. There is no other like him that you will know.

You were given a place to live and care for, and NOW it needs more care. You were given a place to be joyful in, and it needs your joy to overtake the sadness and wrongdoings upon the Earth. It needs your hand in revitalizing all the goodness you were given. You need to spread all the goodness you have to others, and help restore everything and everyone on the Earth. It is time to align with God and become one with the Lord for his tasks are many, and you are many that need restoration and guidance.

Take it upon yourself NOW to help with this restoration process, and be aware that you will attune yourself with God in the process. There is much to do, and it starts with you starting to do something good for another. It starts with you to take the first steps in wanting to do this - seeking out your purpose, seeking God's Word, and turn all of it into actions unto the Lord for he is good and great. His love abounds, and you will feel his love in what you do and say, which is given to you from God.

God is working with many in this restoration process. He feels that the efforts of a few are beginning to make a difference, but he needs everyone to stop what they are doing and do something for God. Help with this restoration process. Help another. Help those in need in some way. Help with what you can do for NOW. God will show you the way(s) you can and will help.

It is a great task to restore the Earth unto itself; to become more whole and fully functioning. Just as we seek restoration, so does the Earth and everything in it. It is ours to take care of and nurture. We were given responsibility to care for the animals, plants, mankind, and everything the Earth offers us. It is a vast task but needs to be looked after and restored.

There is hope in the fullness of a totally restored planet, and it shall be so, says the Lord, with your help and good works. No one is greater than God, and he is within you, so this task is not something you cannot do. It is something you can do with the help of others by your side in like-mindedness. Some will be given gifts to help along the process. Some will be given helpers. Some will be given creativity to figure out problems. Some will want to help with botanicals and restore the waters and seas. Some will want to help mankind to restore their faith and soul. It is all restoration in the eyes of the Lord.

This process is upon you NOW, and you need to act. Do not put your desire to put it aside, but know that your desire to act is stronger for this restoration process is upon you NOW. Many need to be restored, and the time is NOW to start taking it upon yourself to act, and not still be seated in this process.

Walk among you, and see what needs to be done. I am sure just outside your front door is something you can do to help in this restoration process. It is a little help, which leads to a lot of help as a collective. Rejuvenate and restore. Replenish and revitalize. Rebuke the devil and the problems he creates, and rebound with the words of God to banish the evil from the Earth. Relinquish your doubts and hindrances, and repossess what is rightfully yours; that you are of God's nature and he is one with you. He is within you. You are him. You are of like-mindedness. You are of the same spirit and have the power of his nature in you.

Retake what is already there. Renew your faith in yourself. Re-partake the wonders of the Lord. Regret nothing, but work on this restoration. Replenish with joy in your heart and soul. Let the spirit within you shine like your soul is on fire for the Lord and all he stands for. Put this energy to good use in this restoration, and it will make great strides going forward. God awaits your thoughts, decisions, and beginnings of this process within you, and then along with others.

He sees much to be done and is willing to come to you in your time of need. Ask, and it shall be given.

Do not hesitate much. Do not be afraid of what will happen for it is only good that would come from all this work that needs to be done. Do not be rash, but look unto the Lord for help and assistance when needed. Be mindful of others and their separate tasks different from yours that need to be done also. We all have different purposes and need to fulfill them. Be patient and kind. Be diligent and respectful to others and all living things. Be dutiful and partake in the goodness you bring to others while doing all that you do.

It is a restoration of body, mind, and soul. It is a restoration of animals, plants, and all that it is in and on the Earth. It is a task that would be easy for God to do, but it seems it is not going to be done that way. He wants you to partake and give unto others. He gives you no limits on what you can accomplish. He gives you no limits on what good you can do for everything. So, do not limit yourself. Go with God, and be happy, that he is next to you to help you with everything you need help with. Peace and good will to all.

Chapter 20

Substance Is in You

We are here to help you also, so do not be afraid to ask for help from us. We have many specialties that can contribute to your success and wellbeing. We offer our services and aid freely, and hope you will partake of the blessings we offer also. God makes us available to those who need and want the help. We are followers of Christ, Jesus, and will help in every way we can and are able to. We hold much in our power to do good also on the Earth, and with your help, it will be accomplished.

Every day is an opportunity to gain control of the good and spread it to others. We see so much vibrancy on the Earth and know that many are already working for the goodness of others and the Earth in its entirety. Much wisdom comes from those elders that have seen the ways of nature, and the gifts it sustains. Much wisdom comes from those who tend the animals, and seas. Much love comes from those who have given of themselves to treat others with respect and nurturing.

This is a time of restoration and growth, and it is there for the asking and the taking. We all will participate in one way or another to make it so. There is no lack of evidence that the Earth is needing repair, and the people need restoration for all that the people need to do to take care of everyone, and all that the Earth is and has provided. It is to your own benefit to start to think of ways you can help and be a part of a huge restorative project; none like you have ever seen before. Your jurisdiction will be told to you, and your part will be explained in one way or another. Just ask, and you shall receive. It will come to you in thought or word. You will know it is right for the asking and the taking on your part.

Much is accomplished in groups, and many of you will form and be in groups to have an intended goal of restoration. You will enjoy all the company you will have in assisting each other in the tasks you set forth to do. It is a meaningful journey, and it will be allowed to happen for this is the way of the Lord our God. He wants the Earth to be restored and given new life for all to partake and benefit from the Earth's resources and goodness to all. It has much to give the inhabitants, and the time is starting NOW to make yourself aware of your part in this restorative process.

So, wake up to the inner music inside of you that delights in your wellbeing. The music will take you away to a place of knowing and serenity. You will find peace and purpose and come to light with the goodness of God in you. It will show in your face, mannerisms, good nature, and the willingness to help another. It will be your joy of living. It will be a time to rejoice, and also hard work to those who want to accomplish much. We see much in giving. It will be much to behold when so many will be active and doing God's work on the Earth. Store for all to do, and it will be done according to God's plan. This is not a hoax or disillusionment, but a real combining of efforts by many who will succeed in their goals. We are here to help and await your requests for all those who ask will be given answers, the Lord says.

We are not known to everyone on the Earth, but we do help all those who ask for help. We would ask, that our purpose and mission be told to others so that they can ask also. We ask for nothing, but your word of help to aid another. We can offer much, and it will be provided with what we are able to do. So, begin to think of what you would like to do first and foremost to help with this restoration process. There are so many choices, and we can help with that also. We see how busy many of you are doing all that needs to be done already in your life on Earth. It is a formidable task we put upon your shoulders. We know how much work it will be for you. It will be joyful work and not seem so heavy on your shoulders to accomplish all what you set out to do. You will rejoice in the feelings it gives you, and the help it provides to many.

We look upon you as caretakers of the Earth, and God has deemed it so. It is your task to take part in this renewal and restoration process where all will reap the benefits of this accomplishment. Many are waiting to start, so we must begin without haste, and join forces to accomplish much. We know that you will get weary and tired at times. Then, look to us for some comfort and lifting of burdens. We will accommodate your needs in what we are able to do.

This is a journey that God sees as needed and is taking steps to make it so. This is a journey of restoration of the mind, body, and soul to many, so take it seriously and with commitment to others and yourself, since you are a part of the whole. You are a needed cog in the wheel to make this happen. You are needed just like the person next to you. We are all to make a change in the world starting as soon as you are able. The time is NOW to start thinking and doing what you feel is right for you to do.

So, begin with a knowing, a prayer, or a question, and it will be given to you to take the next steps. It will be shown to you or said to you without much hesitation on your part since you will be committed to help others as you will be helped also. We all will make a difference in this world, and God has given you the way to do that. He shows you by this communication that it is needed, wanted, and requested that you partake in this restoration process. It will rejuvenate you. It will empower you to do more and more. It will balance your life out more and make you feel whole, and one with the Earth and all that it contains. It will put you in a place so that you can put your efforts to good use to many and all. It will show others that they need to partake of this journey with you and help all as needed.

We show you what to do with this communication, and ask that you start NOW to speak to the Lord, and he will answer you. God wants you whole. He wants you healthy. He wants you restored in his graces. He wants you to be glad and joyful that you are the sacred one who is inside of you. He will restore and make your life whole and pleasing to others. God is good. God is great. You will know this and act accordingly.

The journey is before you, and it is a great path where you will see changes for the good in mankind. You will see hope and love restored beyond belief. You will see what love can do and has done. You will see many take up with you and add to your duties. It will be an amazing journey, so let us start NOW. Let us begin this new goal of restoration and rejuvenation so we will be more attuned with our heavenly Father. This process will change you and all that are around you, all lands, and all that are on and in the land. Much is to be accomplished, and much will be restored on Earth, so sayeth the Lord. Peace and blessings on you.

Chapter 21

Reach Out and Behold All That Is Yours to Partake

God wants you in his favor. He searches you out to work with you, when you need him. He will work with you for all things that you need with his guidance in mind. He has rules and laws that you will become familiar with as time goes by. You will know when he is not pleased with your actions to others. He will let you know if you are doing well or not, so be alert to the signs around you. You will need to have awareness and be attuned to others around you also. We are all working for the good and grace beings God has dominion over. He wants everyone to be healthy and happy for the good of others, and that is what we all should be working towards.

God is love. He is your Almighty God, who reigns over all the Universe. He aligns himself with you to develop you, and your good graces he has given you. He wants you to succeed and do well for others - all others with no exceptions. We are talking about everything in the Universe - not just human beings; every piece of dust, every piece of water, every piece of mineral deposit, and all the creatures both big and small. We are all of his Universe, and that is how he sees it. God honors them, and you must also honor them. He will ask more of you to be somewhere else after a time. He will let you know.

God favors you and all about you. You have to treat these things about you as such. Precious are these things about you; both in and outside of you. He wants you healthy and happy to lead enriching lives that are exceptional in nature. He looks for much improvement in all of your lives on Earth and extends himself towards you that you may experience what he has for you. Do not be afraid of what is given for you to do, because you will succeed in doing what he asks of you. He cannot wait for you to ask for some will be given their duties or assignments/purpose beforehand. He is eager for all of us to get started and be a part of a reformation of the Earth without a major intervention.

God wants the best for all. He works with everything and everyone to assure that his thoughts and directions are followed. We are many to help and assist you in what you will be doing, and God wants you to know that ahead of time. We are many joining forces with you to give you what you need at the time of need. We grace you when you are not aware of us. We hold you in a still moment of time so that you can recover from something not good for you to have. We watch you laugh and be joyous in each other's company at times. We fulfill your needs even though you do not see us or know us yet. We are by your side, and we are all around you at various times. We sing your praises to God as you do well for him and others. We connect with you if you let or allow us to do so. We watch and wait to be called to assist.

We are all about you and know that we have power of our own under the guidance of the Lord our God. He directs us and commands us at times to do more than before or what we have done before. He stretches us also. You will be stretched if you do what God asks you to do. If you accept what he suggests, then you will become more Christlike in nature. He wants you to be attuned with him and able to speak with him as you want or will. That is a process needed to be learned, and that can happen also if you require it to be so for you. God will let you know if you ask him.

That is the truth as we see it and have related to you in this book. We see that many will be eager to work and some will need proof as to the authenticity of these words. We shall give that proof as needed to each that require it in time. God will respect your decisions and not intervene unless you ask it of him. He is there for you, and you should know that. Much will be done, and it is for you to start when you are ready and willing. We know that you are able, so let us begin together with the help of our Lord the Most High. He attains much, and he expects much, which can and will be fulfilled if you accept him. We would like to start as soon as possible, so if you have no delays, we want you to start with us.

Sit in a quiet space and let your thoughts flow to us, and we will hear you, and make ourselves known to you in various ways. If you are searching for a task to do, put your mind to it, and see if it feels right for you to do. We can help direct you if you need us to do that. So, verbalize what you are needing, and we will help you.

There is a force of love that will develop eventually that will be so strong you will feel it wherever you go, but it is not so developed yet. We see it in the future of the Earth, and it is a resounding clear tone of love and serenity in nature of all of your souls still needed to be developed. All of this will take some time on Earth, and it will be a wonderful journey for many/most to take. We see much pleasure in the tasks and hard work you all will be doing.

So, start as you will, and please everyone as you go. Do what you are needed to do. Rest and restoration will be keywords to take note of. We need rest from the past, and restoration for the future to develop into something better and greater for the good of all and of God's nature. Happy are those who will join us, and sad will be the outcome of others until they begin doing good for others. Much love and blessings about you this day as you read these pages, and wonder what you will be doing next.

Love develops in those who love the Lord. He favors you, and you will know it without reservation one day soon. We are here, and you will know and feel that also. We take your thoughts seriously so be mindful of all that you think, say and do.

Laws of your land are meant to be followed so that peace and harmony will be maintained. Disruptions are not good for the outcome of others, so they are not to happen without consequences in your land. There is justification in land laws and are set up for law and order to be maintained. Even God has laws that have to be maintained. So, respect others and limit your foolishness to only good things for others.

We see the Earth in turmoil daily, and it is for this reason that these changes need to occur. Much will be changed, and much will happen. You may not know what those changes will be right now, but you will see vast changes going forward. Work on your purpose or assignment(s), and you will see great changes one day in you and others around you.

Love and peace, blessings and harmony to you all from all who have contributed to these writings, that you read and take to heart for they are true words left to be fulfilled by you and those around you.

Afterword

A great restoration is about to begin. Much will be gained and restored. Much will happen.

5/30/2020 (Channeled date)

There will be a time of great joy in the nation, and it will be rather soon. There will be a day of forgiveness, repentance, and restoration that will begin this great transformation and it will be soon in the future. We think you know when it will be. The day the book, *God Favors You*, is published? Yes, it will start that day and continue until full restoration is completed sometime in the future. Does this day have a special name? Why yes, it does. It will be called Magnificent Transformation Day in that it will start all of that into motion. It will be celebrated by all in heaven as the definitive mark of when it all begins and is what we all have been preparing for so that the Earth will be in complete harmony again with heaven and the other energy planets and bodies in space and time. It will be the start of a new rejuvenation of all on the Earth. It is coming and will not be delayed any longer.

There will be a time of wonder in the world. It will be a time of no confusion but great miracles and fantastic happenings to many. Life will be preserved and the good graces of God and all above will flow down from the heavens and begin to make the Earth whole, again and again, going forward.

More will be forthcoming as we go along in this journey of restoration, rejuvenation, and re-balancing of everyone and everything on the Earth. So, be aware your future of others is in your hands. Take heed to do what is right for everyone.

Go with God, and he will help you along the way. He is your Light showing you the way to go. He is your Redeemer and will not forsake you. There is no one like him or ever will be. He is the Light and the Truth and the Way. So follow him and be restored again and again. He is on a path of forgiveness, righteousness, and restoration. Be blessed in the Word of God our Creator. It will be a time of need, want, and change. Stand strong and stand with God the Almighty One. Blessings to all who read and follow these messages.

CPSIA information can be obtained
at www.ICGtesting.com
Printed in the USA
BVHW030136210921
617094BV00014BA/343/J

9 781504 396806